THE SPIRIT OF JAPAN

WRITTEN BY
SEAN MICHAEL WILSON

ILLUSTRATIONS BY
FUMIO OBATA

First published in 2021 by Liminal 11

Editors: Sarah Wray and Darren Shill
Art Director: Mike Medaglia

Printed in China

ISBN: 978-1-9126-3423-1

10 9 8 7 6 5 4 3 2 1

www.liminal11.com

LIMINAL 11

CONTENTS

INTRODUCTION:

THE VALUE OF MAGIC
IN EVERYDAY LIVES

What inspired me to think of this book – and then to actually write it – was hearing the common refrain that 'the Japanese are not religious'. I've heard it from a variety of sources, including people in the UK before I ever visited Japan, and from various foreigners in Japan itself. The most extreme example came from a Christian I met several years ago who condemned the Japanese as 'godless' – a declaration which, as with so many clichés, turned out to be full of holes. What an easy world this would be to live in if clichés were more reliable!

I'm from Scotland and presently live in Japan. I first visited Japan almost 20 years ago, and later moved here with my Japanese partner, in part because I thought it would be a good place for our son to grow up. In that time, my study of Japanese history and culture has developed both via personal experience and through the research and writing of more than a dozen manga or graphic novels on Japan. These have been well received, winning a prize in the 2017 International Manga Awards – an annual award organized by the Japanese government – and being nominated for the prestigious Eisner Award in the USA. I have also written many newspaper articles on various aspects of contemporary Japan.

As to my own interest in magic, it came to me via the comic book writers Alan Moore and Grant Morrison, two key creators of the British and American comics which influenced me so greatly as a teenager in Scotland. The inspiration their work placed deep inside me is the reason I went on to become a writer myself. Moore talks of literature, art, music and even language itself as magical acts. In his classic graphic novel with the wonderful Scottish artist Eddie Campbell, *From Hell*, he enshrines this sentiment in a line from a magic-obsessed character: 'The one place Gods inarguably exist is in our minds where they are real beyond refute, in all their grandeur and monstrosity.'[1]

Moore remarked that upon writing those words he stopped and realised that he had unconsciously written something rather profound – and, indeed, true. He decided that he would become a magician, out and out (or in and in). He has noted: 'Magic and Art are the same. Which is why Magic is referred to as The Great Art. They are both technologies of Will, both about pulling rabbits out of hats and creating something where there was nothing.'[2]

Perhaps then, instead of focusing on the word 'religion', if we could use other words – other ways of thinking about it – we may come to a different conclusion. My own preference is to use the word 'magic'; from that perspective, we can see that magical thinking and observances are very much a part of Japanese life. They are part of what we might broadly refer to as 'the spirit of Japan', hence the title of this book, and its subtitle. The vast majority of Japanese partake in various practices which involve some magical aspect. By magic, I mean symbolic acts and beliefs which express and define our relationship with nature, existence and our fellow people. We can find this in everything from marking the new year by burning the old year's objects, to the act of smiling at the rebirth of the sun and admiring new blossoms during spring festivals, to honouring dead ancestors with offerings while chasing demons away.

Over my time in Japan I've attended many of these fascinating – and beautiful – festivals and rituals. It wasn't long before I began to think to myself: if the Japanese are not religious, then what of all these rituals and ancient festivals they have? Don't they have religious origins and aspects?' The first time this was really brought home to me was an occasion on which I brought a large stone into the house. My son's 75-year-old Japanese grandmother reacted with horror, saying 'You can't bring that into the house! It might have negative spirits!' I put it back outside again. Clearly the idea that the Japanese are not religious was wide of the mark.

While the assumption that the Japanese are not religious seems widespread amongst casual observers, further reading revealed I was hardly the only one to suspect otherwise. Michael Pye, professor emeritus at

---

1: Moore, Alan and Campbell, Eddie. *From Hell.*
2: Kaveney, Roz. "Alan Moore: Could it Be Magic?' *The Independent.*

Marburg University and a visiting Research Associate of Otani University in Kyoto has written extensively on the subject of religion, and specifically on aspects of contemporary Japanese religion. A 2008 article of his submits: '… a very specific answer to the question about the sense in which the general population of Japan can be said to be "religious". The question arises because it is frequently denied altogether, especially by Japanese persons themselves. This denial arises because the term "religion", for which there is a Japanese equivalent, namely *shūkyō* (宗教), is widely assumed to imply a very specific belief and value system to which intellectual and emotional commitment is given. It may be admitted that many Japanese persons are not religious in this sense. In another sense however, the vast majority of the population of Japan may be said to be religious in that they participate in a wide range of ritual activity throughout the year which can scarcely be avoided.'[3]

Professor Pye, not being keen on the misunderstandings surrounding the term 'magic', uses the term 'primal religion' to describe much the same thing this book will be focusing on. This serves to differentiate the phenomena from religion such as it is normally thought of. Use of the word 'primal' has some attractive aspects to it as it refers to the radical root of the various activities and perspectives which can be observed in Japan. Though it perhaps serves less well to focus on the everyday nature of the type of activities and thinking under consideration – though Professor Pye certainly does that in the body of his research. Whatever word we give it, the main object of this book is to examine the ways in which the Japanese people engage in religious, magical or supernatural practices and beliefs to the contrary of common opinion – a reality which should be better known and understood.

To that end, this book attempts to provide an accessible but engaging introduction to the subject, focusing not on the fantastical but on the everyday – the aspects which are seen as mundane and 'normal' that most would not label as magical, but which express something sublime and numinous all the same., And while this is neither an academic book nor an exhaustive study of the matter, some effort is made to incorporate vocabulary and viewpoints from related research. Despite their familiarity these practices perform a

---

3: Pye, Michael. "Leading Patterns in Everyday Japanese Religion." *Sphinx, Yearbook 2008-9*: p. 45.

powerful function in dealing with the liminal aspects of death, ageing, time, seasons, nature, etc. Therefore, we can call them 'everyday magic'. Or if you prefer, magick with a k, to differentiate it from the card trick variety.

So, let's look more closely at what we mean by words such as 'magic', 'religion', 'liminal' or 'spirit'. Come to that, what do we mean by 'festival', 'ritual' or 'ceremony'? These are all important phenomena which deeply affect most of us at various times in our lives; yet interpretations of these words can vary, and are sometimes even contradictory. Might one consider communism a religion, for example? According to Yuval Noah Harari it is. In his best-selling book *Sapiens: A Brief History of Humankind* he claims: 'If a religion is a system of human norms and values that is founded on belief in a superhuman order, then Soviet Communism was no less a religion than Islam.'[4] An extreme statement that many have disagreed with, though he does also extend the same logic to capitalism. He goes on to say that if we classify communism or capitalism as ideologies then we should probably also classify Buddhism and Daoism as ideologies too.

So, perhaps the Buddhism and Shintoism of Japan are better classified as ideologies or philosophies rather than as religions. While I do not think it's quite right to say that communism, socialism, anarchism etc. are religions, they do have an undeniable effect on an individual's way of thinking, behaving and relating to other people and the world around them. For now, then, let's put all these phenomena under an umbrella term, and say they are 'Systems of Organisation, Behaviour and Understanding' (SOBU). These magical SOBU affect the way we comprehend the world and our place in it. They influence our politics, workplaces and families as well as our individual and social behaviour, both towards those in our own specific SOBU and those who follow others. And all this manifests in the festivals, rituals and practices which develop as a result, affirmed, recreated and passed on to the next generation. And in this process we are connected to not just the next generation but also the previous ones. As the 'We are the Champions' documentary series on Netflix engagingly phrases it: 'Traditions are a form of magic. Because traditions are a way of talking to the past. Of speaking to our ancestors in a language that they created. When you participate in a tradition, you are casting a spell that lets you talk directly to a bygone era.'[5]

4: Harari, Yuval Noah. *Sapiens*.
5: Erlbach, Matthew-Lee. "We Are the Champions". *Netflix Original Series*.

In considering the mixture of aspects that constitute the Japanese SOBU we also need to take into account the animism that existed in Japan before Buddhism and Shintoism arrived, and which, to a certain extent, still persists today. This blending of influences is the norm. A central tenet of Christianity, for example, is the belief in one all-powerful deity, but believers also pray to hundreds of different saints, who are in some ways not all that different from the pantheistic figures of ancient Greece or Rome with their great arrays of gods for different aspects of life. Likewise, most Christians also have a Christmas tree in their home every year or celebrate Halloween – rituals which date back to pre-Christian animism and magical practices. So, it's not surprising that Japan should also show evidence of such a mixture.

Another point to consider is the relationship between the meanings of the English term 'religion' and the Japanese term *shūkyō*, and how the two became associated – or, more pertinently, how they differ. Is something getting lost in translation? Researcher Mitsutoshi Horii claims: '…the term "religion" was imported to and appropriated as *shūkyō* in Japan in the 19th and early 20th century…the concept was reformulated after the Second World War under the influence of American-style liberal democratic values. To the present day, the boundary between religion (*shūkyō*) and the non-religious secular is ambiguous and often contentious.'[6] He goes on to say that the term *shūkyō* played a key role in the technology of statecraft in late 19th century Japan, but that its usage in everyday modern life is an under-researched area. A series of imperial edicts issued in 1868 set a separation between Shintoism and Buddhism that was not so clear before. Consequently, certain rituals which modern Japan believes to date back thousands of years are actually a far more recent invention. Richard K Payne tell us: 'For example the Shinto wedding ceremony that is familiar today and commonly thought of as an ancient custom was newly created in 1900 for the wedding of the Crown Prince (later, the Taisho Emperor)'[7]

The primatologist Frans de Waal Still suggests the following definition of religion: '…the shared reverence for the supernatural, sacred, or spiritual as well as the symbols, rituals, and worship that are associated with it'.[8]

6: Horii, Mitsutoshi. "Critical Reflections on the Religious-Secular Dichotomy in Japan." Quote taken from the abstract of the paper.
7: Payne, Richard K. "The Ritual Culture of Japan: Symbolism, Ritual and the Arts," in *Nanzan Guide to Japanese Religions*.
8: de Waal, Frans. *The Bonobo and the Atheist*.

These criteria could just as easily fit the word 'magic'; by that reckoning one could say that religion and magic are basically the same thing. However, others would disagree. Those who consider themselves religious in one of the Abrahamic schools may consider it insulting to say that their way is just a form of magic. On the other hand, those who practice various forms of magic may look disdainfully upon the inflexible, hierarchical mainstream religions, which seem to relegate the majority of their followers as passive, rather than active, participants. Why should priests and rabbis be the only ones permitted to 'do' magic?

For the purposes of this book, I would consider magic as essentially 'religion without prohibition'. Magic still concerns the liminal and poetic, but in more a direct and flexible way than is normally associated with religion. For example, religion usually involves an intermediary who does the spiritual work for us; priests who talk to god on our behalf. In magic we have the direct line - we do the spiritual work ourselves. Religion also generally prescribes various prohibitions on action and thought and dress code etc. Magic has less of these, is more open, more focused on what 'works'.

The other thing to note in de Waal's definition is the importance given to the word 'shared'. To return to the idea of SOBU, these are things we do together, in community. The sociologist Émile Durkheim also emphasized the importance of the *shared* experiences of ritual, ceremony and festivals, noting that the intended result is to: 'unite into one single moral community'.[9] This is an integral part of the everyday magic in festivals like *hanami* (花見 flower viewing) or *undōkai* (運動会 school sports day). When Japanese people roll out the blue mats for *hanami* (most people now use a specific thick blue mat, which is in itself an act of community – to mostly use the same style), they come together in a shared act of celebration of spring, food, drink, and each other.

As Moore says, the creation of art – whether it be stories, movies or statues can also be thought of as magical; they reshape consciousness, move us to action, to rethinking, to connecting with other people and to seeing the physical world differently, even to creative work ourselves. Powerful stuff, but still very practical, very everyday. After all, if magic is a way of approaching consciousness then it's something we experience every moment, since we are using magical symbols to consider, express and explore it. Even

9: Durkheim, Emile. *The Elementary Forms of the Religious Life.*

these sentences, the process of me writing them – spelling the words – and you reading them. Don't tell anyone in case they look at you in a funny way, but we're doing magic right now.

So, why did we lovely humans invent magic/religion (or should we say discover it)? It seems that the primary reason was to try to make sense of our world, and to feel that we can affect it in some way – or, at least, feel that we have a two-way relationship with it. The well-known cave paintings of early animal hunts in Lascaux in France and Magura in Bulgaria are artistic portrayals of our world. That in itself is a form of magic, if Alan Moore's remarks about art and language are correct. However, it has also been suggested that these paintings are an evocation of what those early hunters would have liked to happen, rather than a depiction of reality. If so, surely this is an even greater example of magic – a powerful expression of how we would like the future to be shaped by our will.

A very basic question to ask here is: 'Does magic work?' If we say 'can I gain magical powers or summon up protective angels?', then the answer will be probably not (though some say they have done both). But in the sense that the magic of things like art can affect us and our perception of the world so profoundly – in that regard – I think we can say that yes, in some ways magic does work.

This book looks at aspects of how 'magic' of this sort occurs in Japan, through its everyday festivals, rituals, objects, words, actions and places. Despite the title of this book this is not an attempt to capture the essential 'spirit' of Japan, but to show examples of the spiritual or magical aspects that occur. It describes specific examples and examines how, by engaging in these SOBU, people make their lives more meaningful. Ten main festivals and rituals are described and considered, with various examples of additional observances, both ancient and modern, woven into each chapter. I will also explore related issues here and there. Of course, this is not an exhaustive list, and many other elements could be considered, such as *yōkai* (妖怪 ghostly spirits), the debate around secularisation and buddhism, the various new religious cults that have grown up. In addition to all this, we also have the wonderful illustrations of Japanese artist, Fumio Obata, lending their beauty to this book and visualising some of the aspects considered in it.

We magically burn away the old year and collectively count in the new.

NEW YEAR RITUALS

Various rituals take place at New Year (*Oshōgatsu,* お正月) and New Year's Eve (*Ōmisoka,* 大晦日). One such is the building of fires at Shinto shrines. People will burn the charms and amulets (such as *hamaya* 破魔矢 demon-breaking arrows) of the dying year in a symbolic act of ending. Following this, they will go into the shrine to get themselves new charms for the new year. This is a prime example of marking a liminal period, or the changing of one time into another, literally by fire. It's something that's done one way or another in many cultures around the world – but this in particular is an excellent example of magical thinking and practice in Japan. When a person in Japan goes down to the Shinto shrine late in the cold evening of December the 31st to burn a charm from the old year, we can confidently say that magic is working for them.

Or, to use Professor Pye's term, they are engaging in a 'primal religion' that has deep roots in both cultural practice and individual consciousness.

Imagine the scene if you will: it's cold, perhaps gently snowing, the fire burning in the grounds of the shrine draws you in with its appealing primitive glow that connects us to our ancestors. Lots of other people from the local community crowd round. You weave through the crowd to get close to the fire, clutching last year's magical charm in your hand. The heat gets a little too hot on the face as you approach closely and you draw back a bit. Sparks drift up and embers float back down again. It's beautiful and entrancing, but you hope that none of the embers burns a hole in the nice new winter jacket you got from your family on another magical day, Christmas. You step closer again for a moment and cast the charm into the fire, feeling contrasting emotions – you want to get it right into the fire, but don't want to get so close that it becomes dangerous. The charm lands in, and a few moments later begins to twist in the heat, to crackle, to distort...and, as it is consumed, so up with it goes the dying year that has mere minutes left to it... burnt away, symbolically ended.

And now listen – it's the count down, a habit possibly imported from Western countries but now common in Japan:

5,4,3,2,1... wayyhhh!!!

Everyone cheers. Everyone looks at their family and friends. You do too.

A new year starts.

And that's magic. Symbolic magic expressed in common with others, which does something for us, which works.

We could ask 'in what way is it really a *new* year?' It's only time. It's only minutes and hours, weeks and years. Didn't we invent all that? But that's just where the rituals come in. Time is so abstract and artificial that the fire is needed to make it 'real'. The charms are burnt to mark that something has really ended. We need, also, to go to the shrine the next day to buy a new charm, to symbolise this new year. As Franz Kafka, someone much concerned with magical transformation, wrote: '...how for everything, the strangest of things, a great fire is ready...they are consumed and resurrected.'[10] The magical symbolism of burning the charm of the old year, and 'resurrecting' the new year with this year's charm helps us mark the change, cementing the passing of that oh-so-abstract concept, time. Of existence itself.

As Pablo Picasso is believed to have said: 'Everything you can imagine is real.' This may seem a silly statement to some. If I imagine myself with a new red sports car it does not mean one will magically appear on my doorstep. But isn't it true to say that the red sports car I saw drive past me yesterday started in someone's imagination? The imaginations of several people, come to that – those involved in designing and building it. The same applies for intangible and conceptual aspects of our life. A 10 Dollar bill or a Five Pound note have value because we imbue them with value. As part of our financial SOBU, we agree collectively to recognise their worth – to honour the promissory words on them; in reality, they're just pieces of paper

---

10: Hayman, Ronald. K: *A Biography of Kafka.*

with almost no worth at all.

Isn't it much the same with New Year, and birthdays and celebrations of spring? We could argue 'hold on, those events have physical aspects beyond our imagination. They are real.' Yes, *hanami* happens when spring occurs, when the wind catches the falling cherry blossom. We don't imagine the existence of the wind nor invent the force of gravity; but our perception of it, our consciousness of it, and our attitude towards it, are very much the products of our imaginations. Via our SOBU we see beauty in cherry blossoms and snowflakes; we respect the mysterious power of rivers that feed us and sometimes flood us; we appreciate the coming of the sun and the summer crops; we more deeply appreciate the tang of the whisky and the comfort of company if we also clink our glasses together and wish each other good health with the old Gaelic word *slainte*!

So, what are some of the charms or *engimono* (縁起物) used at the turning of the year? My personal favourite is the *hamaya* (破魔矢) – an arrow-like charm about 30 cm. long, decorated with a bell and paper at the end of the shaft so that it makes a charming *ting ting* sound as you carry it home on New Year's Day. The meaning of *hamaya* is 'demon-breaking arrow' or 'demonbusting' as it was – and still is – used to ward off demonic misfortune and attract good luck.

From the Edo period (1603-1868) to the mid-late Meiji period (therefore roughly to the end of the 19th century), these *hamaya* – together with bows – were given as gifts to celebrate the first New Year of a male baby's life. Perhaps the word *hama* derives from an ancient one for an archery target and contest. The use of an arrow alone seems to be a simplified version of this custom. Some people place the *hamaya* arrows (and bows) at the northeast and southwest corners of a new house. These are thought to be directions especially susceptible to evil influences – especially during roof-raising, a type of ceremony performed during the construction of a new building to ensure there are no problems with the new roof.

Other small festivals around this time include *Hatsuhinode* (初日の出) which involves getting up early to watch the first sunrise of the new year. This is clearly a very symbolic piece of magic of the type that humans have surely been taking part in for tens of thousands of years. *Hatsu* means 'first' and *hatsuhinode* therefore means to watch the first sunrise of the year, or literally 'first exit of the sun'. This practice comes from a Shinto tradition which says that *Toshigami* (年神), Year God, the *kami* (神) spirit of the New Year, should be greeted at the first sunrise in order to bring good luck and fine health. A popular place for conducting this ritual – though you have to get up very early in the winter cold! – is at the top of Mount Fuji, though the top of a tall building may also suffice. In addition, the climb up the mountain or the stairs helps to reinforce the effort involved in performing the magic.

Other popular places to experience *hatsuhinode* around the Tokyo area include: Choshi Hill Observatory, known as *Chikyū no Maruku Mieru Oka Tenbōkan* ('Hill Observatory Where the Earth Looks Round') in the town of Chōshi in Chiba Prefecture, which has a 330-degree ocean panorama; Jōnanjima Seaside Park in Ōta Ward, which has a good sea view from Tsubasa Beach; and Miyuki no Hama Beach in Odawara, Kanagawa Prefecture. This last takes its name from an honorific word that denotes the rare 'going out' of an emperor – in 1873, Emperor Meiji and Empress Shoken visited fishermen there. Some brave bathers even take a dip in the freezing waters. Mount Takao is also a popular place to see the sun rise over

The sun coming over the dark old mountain in the distance brings with it the new year and a feeling of liminal change within us.

Tokyo, and has various religious sites scattered across the mountain such as Yakuōin, a Buddhist temple dating back to 744. Tokyo Gate Bridge, also known as Kyōryūbashi ('Dinosaur Bridge') since it looks like two dinosaurs about the duel, has an elevator up to the bridge's sidewalk for a good New Year view.[11]

For those who appreciate the magic of mountains and are willing to make the climb, there exists the ritual of *goraikō* (ご来光), meaning 'the arrival of light'. A 71-year-old Japanese man, who is a private English student of mine, once told me this is his favourite ceremony of the year and that he's never missed it since his father took him on his first *goraikō* in 1954 when he was just five years old. It is associated with a mood of calm, an awareness of the grandeur of nature, of your own connection to it and place within it, and gratitude that you are alive to watch a beautiful sunrise from atop a mountain that is full of life. Mt. Fuji is, of course, the tallest mountain in Japan at just over 3720m above sea level. One can experience a *goraikō* sunrise there during the hiking season from July to the early September.

An interesting point to note here is that, as Richard K. Payne puts it: 'Mt Fuji does not stand for or represent anything, it is just what it is, and as such is sacred in the sense of being a place of great power'.[12] This brings to light a possible difference between Western and Japanese schools of thoughts regarding magical objects as being representative. Payne claims that Japanese religious thinking before the Meiji era was characterised by an absence of such referential symbolism. Instead, previous generations used homologies, thinking in terms of identity between two things that went beyond such 'standing in for' symbolism or simple analogy. James Mark Shields expands on this for us by mentioning the related concept of 'holography': 'Holography refers more directly to the proactive element of the same process—a way of relating to the world, whereby each element or particular of a whole is capable of reproducing or realizing the entirety of the whole.'[13]

The *kami* touched on previously are the spirits, gods, phenomena

---

11: Thomas, Russell. "Hatsuhinode: Where to see the first sunrise of the decade." *The Japan Times.*
12: Payne, Richard K. "The Ritual Culture of Japan: Symbolism, Ritual and the Arts," in *Nanzan Guide to Japanese Religions.*
13: Shields, James Mark. "Beyond Belief: Japanese Approaches to the Meaning of Religion." *Studies in Religion.*

THE SPIRIT OF JAPAN

or holy powers (there is no direct equivalent word in English) of Shinto. As with other animistic beliefs around the world – or SOBU as I have been referring to it – these *kami* are not just human-like figures but also spiritual elements of the environment itself; they are forces of nature in a very literal sense. They are seen as manifestations of an underlying energy of the world, of the universe, called *musubi* (産霊 the spirit of birth and becoming).

If this brings to mind fictional devices such as the Force of the *Star Wars* franchise, there's good reason. George Lucas drew some of his inspiration from a variety of Japanese stories and myths, as well as the wider background of Buddhism, Taoism, Zen and martial arts. For example, the force seems strongly related to the idea of *chi,* or *ki,* found in Chinese and Japanese martial arts, and within Taoism and Zen: 'In the Japanese martial art of Aikido, effortless action is of the essence. The name "Aikido" means the way (*dō*) of harmonizing or unifying (*ai*) the ch'i (*ki* energy and spirit). In order to use the *ki* one must let go of effort... When Obi-wan begins to teach Luke the Way of the Force, he says "A Jedi can feel the force flowing through him."'[14]

Another New Year's ritual is *Joya no Kane* (除夜の鐘 temple bell ringing), practised on New Year's Eve. This is one of my personal favourites for the simple reason that it makes a great *dong* sound when you give a good swing with the wooden beam on a rope and strike the bell. It feels a bit like a fairground game. These large bells are known as *bonshō* (梵鐘 buddhist bells), *tsurigane* (釣り鐘 hanging bells), or *ōgane* (大鐘 great bells) and are found in Buddhist temples throughout Japan. The bell is rung 108 times, one strike for each of the worldly desires/anxieties described in Buddhism, and people will visit their local temple on New Year's Ever to participate. The ringing starts in the evening and goes on to midnight, with one final strike after the new year begins. There's usually quite a queue to get a turn, so you might want to go early if you want to ring that ding! *Joya no Kane* is yet another very old custom, thought to have first started in the Sung Dynasty in China (420-479). It crossed over to Japan along with Zen Buddhism in the Kamakura era (鎌倉時代, 1185–1333). Originally, Japanese Zen temples would ring the bells every day (which might have gotten to be a bit much);

14: Decker, Kevin and Eberl, Jason. *Star Wars and Philosophy: More Powerful than You Can Possibly Imagine.*

the bells were also used for military communication in times of war. Later, bell ringing came to be practiced only on New Year's Eve, and some other rare occasions such as at *Obon* (お盆) time in mid-August.

Even if you don't get to ring the bell yourself the sound of it reverberates around the local area, connecting all who can hear it. The sound is thought to be useful for inducing a meditative state. There are thought to be 3 aspects, or stages, to this. The first is called *atari* (アタリ), the clear tone made upon the initial impact. This followed by the more prolonged *oshi* (オシ), a reverberation of a higher pitch which lasts for up to ten seconds. Lastly the *okuri* (オクリ), a decaying resonance that is heard as the vibrations die away, which can last as long as a minute.

The shape of the bells is considered to resemble the sitting Buddha (sloped shoulders and flat base). As a result, it is customary to bow three times before the bonshō as a sign of respect, much as one should before a statue of Buddha. The oldest of these bells has been dated to around 600 AD, although many note the similarity of the design to that of even older bells in China, which presumably influenced the Japanese ones. Some of the bells used are of considerable cultural and symbolic importance. For example, the bell at Hannyaji temple, at Nara-zaka in the northern part of Nara City, is dated to 1275, and the temple itself to at least 742. It was designated a national treasure during World War II in order to save it from being melted down for the war effort, though it was later 'demoted' to an Important Cultural Property. It is thought that as many as 70,000 ancient bells were melted down during this period, marking a significant loss to the cultural richness of Japan when considered alongside the millions of old buildings destroyed by bombing. Therefore, it seems only right that the surviving ancient bells are so venerated.

Toshikoshi soba (年越し蕎麦) is the tradition of eating soba noodles on New Year's Eve. It is thought to have become common during the Edo era (1603-1868). he long shape of the noodles is said to represent a long and healthy life, while the cutting involved in the making of the noodles symbolizes a desire to cut away the misfortunes of the old year. Chop chop!

Kadomatsu, meaning pine gate, are intricate and attractive displays placed in pairs, representing male and female, outside homes, normally at the house entrance or garden gate. These are intended to welcome the *Toshigami*

THE SPIRIT OF JAPAN

sama (the word *sama* is an honorific denoting respect) in the hopes that they will bless that location for the coming year – something once believed to increase the likelihood of a good harvest for the new year. This custom dates back to the 8th century, and like the bells, is thought to originate in China. After January the 15th (or the 19th) the *kadomatsu* are burned to appease *Toshigami* and release them again. You might notice that I've already mentioned a burning ceremony on New Year's Eve and now I'm mentioning another one around the middle of January. This latter ritual is called *dondo* yaki (どんど焼き) and is focused on securing good fortune for the future. The New Year's Eve burning is called *otakiage* (お焚きあげ) and is more concerned with cleansing oneself of the year that is ending.

A tradition around this time is *otoshidama* (お年玉), which kids look forward to eagerly because they receive special small envelopes of cash for the occasion! They get this from parents, grandparents and other close relatives. The customary amount is normally around 5,000 Yen ($50/£25), though this increases as they get older and quite a lot of college students still receive it. Amounts such as 4,000, 8,000, etc. are not given as they are thought to represent bad luck in much the same way as rooms with the number 304 do, hence many apartment blocks in Japan omit them altogether. Four is considered bad luck because it is sometimes pronounced *shi*, which is also the sound for the word meaning death (死). Another example is that hospitals often avoid having a room four, and especially bed 43, because that could mean still-birth (*shizan* 死産). So, four is often pronounced as *yon* instead. The tradition of *otoshidama* started with the giving of rice cakes to the *Toshigami sama*. Later this changed to the giving of toys, and has nowadays evolved into gifts of money.

There are several types of envelopes for different occasions, such as weddings. The New Year money is given in envelopes called *otoshidama bukuro* (お年玉袋) which are rather pretty, being decorated with bows and illustrations of New Year symbols or characters popular with kids. It is considered rude to give money unwrapped and the cultural equivalent of any adult simply handing the kids a fiver from their wallet would be roundly criticised by others. It's hard to imagine that happening in the West, and is a good example of how Japan conducts itself with a more formal culture than that of the UK or USA. I remember an uncle from the west coast of Scotland who would slip me some money in an almost conspiratorial way when he came over to visit us in Edinburgh. This was presumably done so as not to seem ostentatious by giving me money in a big public display. It also represented a kind of chummy closeness. Not so in Japan. There the giving is formalised, done in public and acknowledged with due respect. The envelopes are not even opened in the presence of the giver, but later in private.

Lastly, there are various food related new year habits such as the *Nanakusa no sekku* (七草の節句 Feast of Seven Herbs of Health) rice porridge eating ritual on January the 7th, which has seven herbs in it, and is said to help calm or balance the stomach after the over-eating of new year's time. This, like many of the magical habits considered here, has a long history, going right back to practices rooted in third century Southern China. The seventh day of the new year was assigned to humans (the other of the first eight days go to pigs, horses, chicken, dogs, sheep, rice and cows). The mix of herbs was thought to help with living a long life, warding off evil and health in general. The seven herbs are basically wild growing and consist of these: chickweed, radish, turnip, nipplewort, cudweed, Japanese parsley (sometimes known as Chinese celery), and shepherd's purse (which is, incidentally, the second-most prolific wild plant in the world). Ingredients differ a bit in various regions. For example, in Kumamoto Prefecture, where I now live, the tradition is to include *mochi* (rice cakes).

As time went on the process of making this magic broth became more ritualized. It became customary to pick the plants the day before, dress up in formal clothes for its preparation, and use traditional cooking utensils. While chopping them people stood in a direction considered to bring good luck. They sang a song, which also differed from region to region, but normally went something like: 'Before the birds of the Tang country fly to Japan, I grind these seven herbs.'

For those who want to try to make this new year meal for themselves please be careful because Japanese parsley (*Oenanthe javanica*) looks very much like toxic water hemlock, which can be very dangerous.

It's interesting to observe the way in which Shinto, Buddhist, Christian and pagan influences all play a part in the celebrations at the end of the year, weaving together in a seemingly frictionless way. Throughout December Christmas lights, Christmas trees, images of Santa, snowmen and other ostensibly Western staples are often seen. After Christmas, however, these suddenly disappear, replaced by trappings of Shintoism such as the *kadomatsu* (門松 pine gate, a traditional Japanese New Year's decoration) and *kagami mochi* (鏡もち a New Year's decoration made of rice cake), or Buddhist traditions like the aforementioned bell-ringing. This blending of roots is perhaps related to the stereotype noted earlier, that the Japanese are not religious. To someone of strict faith it may seem odd, even shallow, to mix various SOBU like that. Observing the traditions of just one SOBU is generally the accepted practice of followers. But in Japan, the mixing of SOBU is far more characteristic than in many other cultures.

OUT DEMONS!
SETSUBUN (節分) BEAN THROWING

Setsubun (節分) is a rather cute festival focused around children, but with its roots deep in a magical practice going back centuries. The name consists of two words: *setsu*, which means 'season', and *bun*, which means 'division'. Therefore, *Setsubun* means seasonal division. It is celebrated on February 3rd as part of the Spring Festival. One component of this is the *mamemaki* (豆撒き bean scattering) ritual, the purpose of which is to chase away evil spirits at the beginning of Spring. It's a fun ritual, engaged in by millions of families each year and particularly enjoyed by kids.

So, what happens? In order to magically usher in the change of the seasons, the ritual of *mamemaki* is performed by throwing *fukumame* (福豆 lucky roasted soybeans) out the door. Alternatively, *fukumame* can also be thrown at a person wearing the mask of an *oni* (鬼 demon) who is symbolizing the evil spirits (it's usually Dad or an uncle). People excitedly chant 'Evil out! Good luck in!' (*Oni wa soto! Fuku wa uchi!* 鬼は外! 福は内!) during this ritual. It's good fun. My own son really liked it when he was a boy.

Afterwards, a common habit is to eat one roasted soybean for each year of your life. There is also *ehōmaki* (恵方巻), a kind of rolled sushi of the *makizushi* (巻き寿司) type known as *futomaki* (太巻). There's certainly an aspect of magical thinking to the idea that it will bring good luck when eaten (whole, with your eyes closed) while facing in a certain direction dictated by the Chinese zodiac. Sardines are also eaten on Setsubun, another good example of the mundane in magical practice as their smell is considered to ward off evil spirits. An interesting extension on this belief, though I don't think I've seen it myself, is a distinctive decoration called *hiiragi iwashi* (柊鰯), a wreath made

Dads and Uncles often dress up demons at Setsubun time – great fun for the kids to pelt them with beans!

from sardine heads and holly leaves.[15]

The official start of Spring is noted as *Risshun* (立春 on February 3rd or 4th), which is also the beginning of a new year in Japanese lunar calendar. The Chinese calendar was introduced to Japan via Korea in the middle of the sixth century. A.O. and P.P. Scheffler. claim that the Japanese and Chinese calendars are virtually identical: '...the main difference, being that besides the cyclical dating and chronology being tied to the reign of each emperor [Japanese emperor to Japanese calendar; Chinese emperor to Chinese calendar], a general year numbering system [was] used that dates from the Emperor [of Japan] Jimmu Tennō in 660 B.C.'[16] It has been noted, however, that there are small differences which mean a disparity of a day or two, or sometimes more.

This lasted for more than a thousand years until 1685 when the calendar was adjusted to consider various Japanese aspects. Then, in 1873, the Gregorian calendar was adopted as part of Japan's modernization. People in the UK in the early 1970s complained of adjusting to a 'new money' system, so think what it must be like to adjust to a whole new way of measuring time!

In modern Japan, the old Chinese calendar isn't paid much mind, save by Chinese and other Asian immigrants. However: 'In modern times, many of the aspects of the "old" lunar system remain in Japanese culture including determination of some festivals and observances (such as *Tanabata* on the seventh day of the seventh month), names for years after the current Emperor (1996 is Heisei 8), and the old Chinese sexagesimal and astrological associations (familiar animals such as mouse, cow, cat, rabbit, etc.). While many Japanese faithfully continue to plan events with their "supplemental" lunar calendars, the Gregorian system is officially recognized for all legal transactions.'[17]

Another example of the casting out of demons and bad luck is the car safety blessing ritual *kōtsū anzen* (交通安全). This magical practice is not unique to Japan, but common across much of Asia. The Ganesh Temple at Benagluru in India, for example, is a popular place for traditional car and motorcycle

---

15: Wada, Teni. "Setsubun: The Japanese Festival of Bean Throwing and Sushi Rolling," *Kokoro Cares*.

16: Scheffler, A.O. and Scheffler, P.P. *CalMaster2000: Dates, Holidays, and Astronomical Events*.

17: Renshaw, Steve and Saori Ihara. "The Lunar Calendar in Japan." *Renshaw Works*.

blessings. In Japan the Shinto priest, called a *kannushi* (神主), bows before the vehicle and again to the owner if they are standing next to it, then waves an wand called an *ōnusa* (大幣) or *haraegushi* (祓串), a wooden baton with long white paper tassels or streamers on it. They do this four times: twice from right to left, and twice from left to right, before bowing twice more. They then go to the open right-hand door of the vehicle and perform the same blessing with the *Ōnusa* there too, in order to purify the interior. Sometimes they'll even bless the back of the car as well.

    The *ōnusa* wand makes a satisfying swishing sound as it's waved by the *kannushi*. As with the New Year's bells, this sound – subtle and soft though it is – is a key part of its ritual. The paper attached to it allows us to feel, or hear, the magic happening. One of my Japanese students is a scientist, yet he told me he always has this car cleansing ceremony performed when

An interesting meeting of the old and the new: a new car being given a Shinto blessing.

he buys a new car. There's a similar magical ritual that is performed for new houses and plots of land.

Another concept worth considering is that of *kotodama* (言霊 word magic). We are of course, as I said, doing word magic right now, as I write this and as you read it. The essence of the *kotodama* philosophy is to revive our awareness of the astonishing magic of language – or, at least, to remind us to reflect on it from time to time, which is better than blindly taking this amazing thing for granted. By centring around the soul of language, this practice presupposes that sounds can magically affect objects, people and the environment. The power in words can affect our body and mind, and even – if such a thing exists – our soul.

This certainly seems to be the case. If you approach a stranger who's wearing the t-shirt of some sports team and say: 'Hey, that team is terrible!', you are likely to provoke a bad response. But if you say 'Hey, I'm a fan too!' instead, the response is far more likely to be positive. That's obvious – so why mention it? Because that's exactly what the *kotodama* philosophy is focusing on. It's looking at how words produce change in us and in the world. The decision to cut down that section of a forest, for example, will normally come about as a result of some pronouncement, a judgement that has been taken, a law that has been passed. Words cut down trees. They also produce nuclear reactors, and solar panels. They start wars, or end them. Words are scary things! Be careful with that axe, Eugene. It can build or it can kill.

Community spirit is created and reinforced in the dancing, the dressing up, and the 'musicking' of *Obon* time.

OBON (お盆) ANCESTORS

Obon (お盆) or just *Bon* (盆) is an annual Buddhist event for commemorating the spirit of one's ancestors. It is believed that each year during *Obon*, the ancestors' spirits return to this world in order to visit their relatives. This makes it somewhat similar to Samhain, Dia de Muertos or Halloween as celebrated in various other cultures (though *Obon* happens in the heat of August, rather than the chill of late October). And, as with Halloween, the festival can involve dressing up as ghosts and demons and having fun!

The festival is thought to be a mixture of Buddhist and Confucian customs of more than 500 years' standing which has its origin in the Ghost Festival of China, itself a combination of the Buddhist *Ullambana* and the Taoist *Zhongyuan* (中元). The word Obon is therefore a shortened form of *Ullambana* (于蘭盆會) or *Urabon'e* (盂蘭盆會), which is in turn derived from the sanskrit meaning 'hanging upside down'. This could be seen as reminiscent of The Hanged Man tarot card, which is associated with suffering. By cleaning the graves of the ancestors, thereby showing them due respect in the process of returning home, this could be seen as an effort to reduce their suffering.

Today, *Obon* is primarily a family reunion holiday. During this time people make the journey back to their hometowns, sometimes making long treks from distant cities. In this respect it's also rather like Christmas or New Year in Western cultures. The graves of ancestors are visited, food offerings are made at house altars and temples, and lanterns are hung in front of houses to guide the ancestors' spirits. Likewise, in many places floating lanterns are put into rivers, lakes and seas in order to guide the spirits back to their world to mark the end of *Obon*. The magical significance of the festival's goals is clear: connecting with family lineage and placating the spirit world.

The most important part of *Obon* is visiting the graves of one's ancestors, which are often at some distance from the family home, and cleaning them with a simple magic ritual. A brush is used to wash away dirt or stains on the stones and around the graves; following this, the stones are rinsed using a special pail of water and ladle. The ground is neatly swept, and incense candles are carefully placed. The family will then say some prayers for the ancestors, both for those they actually remember and for the ones distanced by time whom they never met.

The 2019 anime *Weathering with You* (*Tenki no Ko* 天気の子) directed by Shinkai Makoto depicts the performance of an *Obon* ritual. In it an old lady, Tachibana, performs a simple but powerful magical ritual at Obon time with a 15-year-old-girl, Hina: 'She conducts a ritual burning of a small ceremonial bonfire (*mukaebi* 迎え火) to welcome the souls of her ancestors, so that her late husband can come back, carried by the smoke from the fire. She encourages Hina to walk across the small bonfire, so that she can be protected by the soul of her mother who had died the previous year'[18]. There are various important aspects going on here. The old lady acts as a 'wise old person' archetype as Joseph Campbell tells us in his classic book 'The hero with a thousand faces'. She helps the lost and troubled Hina connect with a sense of community, with the past and with nature via the ceremony. *Obon* is a truly special time, both in facilitating connection with the departed, and in the positive effect it has on the living.

Writer Amy Chavez notes: 'It's hard not to agree that *Obon* is a beautiful tradition. It brings family together from all over the nation and further unites them with siblings, cousins, parents, grandparents, great grandparents and all those before them. But the biggest beneficiaries are probably the ancestors themselves, who get to meet and spend time with family old and new, even if just spiritually'[19]. This is a key element of what magic does for us: it helps to create community, forging bonds through the rituals and festivals and specific habits entailed. The benefits of this may, according to Chavez, even extend back in time...

A traditional dance performed at this time – the *Bon odori* (盆踊り) the *Bon* festival dance) – was originally a *Nenbutsu* folk dance (Buddhist incantation using chanting, drumbeating and dancing) intended to welcome

---

18: Yoneyama, Shoko, "Rethinking Human-Nature Relationships in the Time of Coronavirus: Postmodern Animism in Films by Miyazaki Hayao & Shinkai Makoto." *Asia Pacific Journal*.
19: Chavez, Amy. "Five things you need to know about Obon." *Japan Today*.

the spirits of the dead. Chavez points out that these serve a ceremonial purpose as well as that of entertainment: 'The Shiraishi Odori has been performed for over 700 years and was used as a vehicle to pray for the souls of the fallen warriors in the sea battles of the Genpei Wars (1180-1185). It is still performed every day of the Bon period for this purpose and is a designated National Intangible Cultural Property in Japan.'[20]

Such festivals and practices are often linked back to significant periods of warfare. The fact that these are still performed hundreds of years later demonstrates the impressive role that such magical activity plays in creating cultural continuity; though in some cases, such as that of the infamous Yasukuni Shrine in Tokyo or the horse festival in Kumamoto show, these cultural staples are sometimes the source of contention with China and North and South Korea, which view the military aspects involved as an ongoing insult. The very lively (and even rather dangerous) Kumamoto horse festival used to be called '*Boshita Matsuri*' and was connected with the victory over Korea in the 16th Century. In the late 1980s, however, the name was altered to 'Great Festival of Fujisaki Hachimangū Shrine' following a campaign by Koreans and Japanese of Korean descent to have it changed. This was largely successful in decoupling the festival from its militaristic origins, and it still takes place every year during September. Visitors can spectate and, if they are part of a local group, even participate.

Together, horses and dancers move through traffic and excitedly shout out their chant of *dōkai! dōkai!* (どーかい！どーかい 'How was it? What did you think?') which some think is derived from the original meaning of 'How was the sex?' The older chant used prior to the event becoming more politically correct was *boshita! boshita!* (ぼした！ぼした！), which is thought to be derived from the word *horoboshita* which was used to chant that Japan destroyed Korea, hence the campaign for change in the '80s.

Yasukuni Shrine in the Chiyoda area of central Tokyo is probably one of the best-known, and controversial, shrines, owing to the criticism it often receives from abroad. Whether or not a Japanese Prime Minister chooses to visit it is often taken as a sign of how tough they are going to be in their relations with China and the two Koreas. The shrine was founded by the Emperor Meiji in 1869 and was originally intended to commemorate those who died in the Boshin War (1868–1869), but this purview has since

---

20: *Ibid.*, Chavez.

expanded all the way through to the volunteer Japanese soldiers who fought in the First Indochina War (1946–1954). Visitors may be enticed to visit the shrine thanks to its notoriety, but should be aware that doing so may be frowned upon. In 2014 the singer Justin Bieber was strongly criticized for posting a photo of himself at the shrine. He later said he didn't know about the contentious aspects and thought it was 'merely' a religious place. For those who do wish to visit, the shrine has its own *Obon*-type festival in mid-July every year called *Mitama Matsuri* (みたままつり Mitama Festival). During the festivities, the entry walkway is decorated with impressive 40-foot-high walls of more than 30,000 glowing yellow lanterns, and is a popular event for locals.

Beyond the wider political connections of these magical places and celebrations, the dancing and singing is perhaps the part of the *Obon* festival that people in their twenties enjoy most – especially as it's sometimes thought to be a good way to meet a partner. That said, *Obon* is an event for people of all ages; it's very much a cross-generational festival. Due to being in the height of summer, people wear lightweight *yukata* (浴衣 an informal summer garment) or light jackets called *happi* (法被 a straight sleeved coat worn during festivals), along with special fans, traditional *geta* (下駄 a form of traditional Japanese footwear resembling flip-flops) or *tabi* (足袋 traditional socks), and sometimes quite elaborate headwear, such as the *amigasa* (編笠 straw hat). Special dances are performed, subtle but highly prescribed, with everyone performing the same style in long lines as they march through their city or over sacred grounds. Drums (*taiko* 太鼓) and a type of Japanese zither (*koto* 琴) instruments are also played and the groups are separated into *ren* (連), which often have their own style of dress.

Many regions have their own versions of this dance, and different songs to go with it. In this way, rituals and festivals help to create and maintain social unity and a sense of community. By passing on these traditional styles of dance and song, older and younger people are able to connect in a venerated ceremony of very long standing – one which is fun, active, and a real event in the yearly calendar. Many people come to watch and enjoy, and to take part in *communitas*; something Scottish anthropologist Victor Turner placed much importance upon: 'Communitas refers to an unstructured state in which all members of a community are equal, allowing them to share a common experience, usually through a rite of passage. Communitas is characteristic of people experiencing liminality together. This term is used to distinguish the modality of social relationship from an area of common living.'[21]

Hokkaidō has an *Obon* song known as *Sōran Bushi* (ソーラン節). Gifu Prefecture has the *Gujō odori* (郡上おどり) which is famous for the all-night dancing. In the far southern island of Kyushu, there is the *Ohara Bushi* (おはら節) of Kagoshima. Perhaps the best known is the song of Tokushima in Shikoku (the smallest of the four main islands in Japan) with its *Awa odori* (阿波踊り). This festival is thought to attract around a million visitors in the middle of August and takes place over three or four days! *Awa* is what the Tokushima Prefecture used to be called before the Meiji era, and *odori* simply means 'dance', so the *Awa odori* is a bit like the naming a dance the Harlem Shuffle or the Charleston.

The song associated with *Awa odori* is called *Awa Yoshikono* (阿波よしこの), or 'Fool's Dance', and dates back over 400 years. This nickname comes from the lyrics to a common song the dancers sing: 'Fools dance and fools watch... if both are fools, you might as well dance'. Of course, the tarot card The Fool has a deeper meaning than simply that of a clown: it can be seen as the start of something new, a joyful stepping into the unknown, a rebellious expression of celebration. The *Obon* dancers in Japan could be seen in the same way – the dressing up, public displays, dancing, music and so on being as they are a liminal step beyond the straight-laced behaviour of normal life. Indeed, in the uncertain time of the late Edo period as it lurched into the Meiji Restoration , there were some infamous dancing and music celebrations called *ejanaika* (ええじゃないか) (meaning 'who gives a damn!' or 'whatever you like!') that went much further in their visceral mixture of sexual debauchery, politics and violence.

Likewise, in the 17th century, Awa's three days of *Bon-odori* were a major disruption to the normal function of the local area, and rules were drawn up regarding behaviour during the celebrations. The need for these implies that the samurai had been brawling and acting in less than honourable ways prior to their existence. In 1674, they forbade dancers or spectators from carrying swords or poles. In 1685, revellers were prohibited from dancing after midnight and from hiding their faces in any way that prevented

21: Turner, V. (1974). *Dramas, Fields, and Metaphors: Symbolic Action in Human Society. Cornell University Press.* pp. 273-4.

the authorities from identifying troublemakers. Visitors hoping to see some of that action nowadays may be disappointed, though! One key modern characteristic of Japan is a notable lack of large-scale violent protests. There has been nothing like the 2020 protests across the USA or Hong Kong in Japan since the 1960s. It is contentious as to whether this is a good thing or not.

So, having examined some of the better-known *Obon* practices and the purpose they serve, here's a question: does the *Obon* family and ancestor ritual have any effect on keeping families together? If so, how might we measure that? One simple way might be divorce rates. According to data from the Statistics Bureau of Japan, the divorce rate in Japan is 1.7 per 1,000 people.[22] Compared to the U.S. divorce rate of 2.5 per 1,000 people, the former is indeed notably lower. Do these family-centric rituals have anything to do with this? I asked some Japanese friends and acquaintances for their opinions and most said yes, they thought they did. As shared with me by Yukiko Kaikita: 'Rituals and festivals including *Obon* cleaning are sometimes troublesome to me, but still keep families together, I think. Also those things help connect not only family members, but also it's a kind of bond for the community.'[23]

When people divorce, is attendance of the previous family's grave cleaning at *Obon* time continued? Could, for example, a woman still join in cleaning the graves of her ex-husband's family? According to the people I spoke with that would be unusual. When you're out, you're out. This exclusion from that *Obon* ritual could be seen as a symbolic act: since we are divorced you are no longer welcome at this event which celebrates and cements the family unit.

There are, of course, numerous reasons why people get divorced and I am not suggesting that anyone should follow a religion in order to avoid it! We may also consider that a tight family group may also be seen as a constricting institution, imposing 'harmony' in a way that holds its members back in various ways. After the American occupation of Japan following WWII, a new Constitution was established and the Civil Code was revised, including changes to the family, which: '…includes a long catalogue of

---

22: Statistics Bureau of Japan. "Statistical Handbook of Japan 2020".
23: Kaikita, Yukiko. Interview by author, January 2020.

individual rights provisions, designed to protect the individual from the exercise of public power. These articles are incompatible with the cultural ideology of group orientation, hierarchy, harmony, consensus, and loyalty to the group.'[24] That is, however, starting to move a bit too much beyond the scope of this book. The main point here is that the rituals, magical practices and ceremonies probably play some part in cementing family bonds and, indeed, community bonds.

All this focus on ancestors in *Obon* and other rituals may surprise some who think of Japan as a high-tech, future-facing place. This is another common cliché which turns out to only be half-true at best. It's common for people abroad to imagine a place of robots and flashing neon lights and the latest beeping gadgets in everyone's hands. As a British person living here, I

24: Marfording, Annette. "Cultural Relativism and the construction of culture: An examination of Japan." *Human Rights Quarterly.*

Contrary to its hi-tech image, many banks and post offices are still paper-based.

regularly get comments from people back home like: 'Wow, Japan! What a high-tech world you must live in.' Well, no.

Granted, Japan may have the most robots in the world, including the much-trumpeted Pepper from SoftBank which is even supposed to be able to read human emotions. But even in these areas, they're falling behind. The Robotics Society of Japan notes that up until 2000, the country produced around 90% of all robots in the world; but that the figure has now declined to about 60%. In terms of everyday life, Japan is actually rather old-fashioned, still. Walk into almost any post office, bank or estate agent and the non-Japanese visitor may be taken aback by the extensive use of labor-intensive, paper-based systems in place of computers. But, actually, this widespread lack of the high-tech in the day-to-day is, for the most part, just fine. Why do we need a visit to the post office to feel like we are stepping into a scene from *The Matrix*? As long as the lovely, polite staff help us fill out the form, or gently place our package down on the (very old) weighing scale with a friendly smile, well, isn't that enough?

JIZO (地蔵) ROADSIDE SHRINES

You won't have to walk far in Japan before you come across a miniature roadside shrine with a small statue in it. These are called *jizō* or, to use the full honorifics, *Ojizō sama* (お地蔵さま). These are of ancient origin, stretching back at least as far as the eighth century.

Originating in India as the *bodhissatva Kshitigarbha*, they spread with Buddhism first to China, then to Korea and finally to Japan. *Jizo* became not only an object of worship, but also one of the most beloved and popular divinities in the country. His main purpose then was to watch over travellers and children – therefore they often have cute bibs and/or hats. Most of the *jizō* statues you see today date back to the Edo period (1603-1867). By a comical coincidence, in my home country of Scotland 'jizo' is a slang phrase meaning 'oh my god!', used to express exasperation at some trouble.

As can be seen from the fresh clothes they wear and the small oranges or cups set down for them, these *jizō* statues are still looked after – often by an elderly person living nearby. They look after the bibs that are often placed around the necks of the *jizō* and place mikan oranges at the shrines as offerings. Recently in preparation for a storm I saw one such old woman closing off the wooden gates of a large stone frame which housed a *jizō*. I stopped to talk to her and thanked her for looking after this local statue. She was surprised that a foreigner knew or cared about *jizō*, but was pleased that I had stopped to show appreciation of her effort. Sometimes I wonder if these statues will still be cared for, say, 50 years in the future. I think they will for the most part. There are a great number of them; estimates put this number at around a million in total. I personally know of at least a dozen within about four kilometers in any direction of where I live, and almost all of these are regularly maintained.

It's been reported that the use of *jizō* has now spread beyond Japan, particularly as a symbolic magical figure for people who have lost children.

Japan has around 1 million *jizō* statues dotted around streets and small enclaves..

The writer Angela Elson wrote in the *New York Times* about her miscarriage and how focusing on her *jizō* helps her and her partner: '*Jizō* now sits and reminds us of the baby we lost – not so often as to make us sad, but often enough so that we don't forget him entirely.'[25] The article had many comments from other grieving parents for whom a *jizō* statue was performing a similar, bolstering role. This is another heart-warming example of how magic can do something for us and help us in our lives. Elson also mentions that one of the reasons they turned to a *jizō* was the lack of any equivalent in the USA: '…maybe it was the lack of traditions surrounding miscarriage in the States that gave me nothing to take the edge off my grief. Without a prescribed course for mourning, I didn't know what else to do besides mother this lump of concrete as if he could actually transfer my love to the afterlife.'

Perhaps that lack of tradition applies mostly to the Americans of European descent; in Ireland, however, it is quite common to see small roadside shrines to the Virgin Mary, and I wonder whether any Irish Catholics brought that tradition with them to the USA. Indigenous Americans have various death rituals which may fulfil the same role that the *jizō* took on for Elson's family. For example, the Oneida Nation who come from the area now known as New York: 'One modern practice by the Oneida Nation is the Community Death Feast. These annual feasts are held once each spring and once each fall to honor those who have died. Each person in the community brings a traditional food like corn mush, wild rice, or venison to share with the whole group. One plate is filled with some of each shared dish and placed in a private area just before sunrise as a token for the dead.'[26] For some, that death festival, performed with others in community, may assist them in overcoming loss. For Elson and her family, it was the more private use of the *jizō* of Japan.

A famous example of *jizō* statues popular with foreign visitors is the lovely row at the Zōjōji Temple in the Minato area of Tokyo. However, as with most of the festivals and rituals under consideration, *jizō* can be found all over Japan, so it's not really appropriate to single out any one place to go. If you want to see a *jizō* statue, just take a stroll in almost any urban area, and you are highly likely to come across one within 10 or 15 minutes. You could even adopt it as your own local *jizō* and maybe leave a mikan orange there.

25: Elson, Angela. "The Japanese Art of Grieving a Miscarriage." *New York Times*.
26: Meleen, Michele. "Native American Death Rituals." *Love to Know.*

Buddhist tree-burials, *jumokusō*, are becoming more popular – beautiful and ecological.

FUNERAL AND DEATH RITUALS

The vast majority of people in Japan are cremated: and despite the Japanese people's reputation for not being religious, most of these funeral ceremonies are overwhelmingly Buddhist ones. Most houses here have a small Buddhist altar, or *butsudan* (仏壇). When a death occurs, the doors of the shrine are closed and it is covered with white paper to keep out bad spirits. A small table decorated with flowers, incense and a candle is often put near the dead person's bed.

'An ancestral grave is almost systemically associated with its complementary family altar (*butsudan* 仏壇). Located in the home, the altar is usually a wooden cabinet which contains the Japanese Buddhist mortuary tablets (*ihai* 位牌) of deceased members... In addition to the memorial tablets, the altar contains various objects such as religious iconography, statues, prayer sheets, lanterns, various offerings, a ritual bell to summon the ancestral spirits and other such ritual objects.'[27]

Care is taken to decide an auspicious time for the funeral, depending on magical considerations of the old Chinese six-day lunar cycle. The body is ritually washed and the orifices are blocked with cotton or gauze. Deceased women are dressed in a white kimono and men in a Western-style suit or kimono. Certain items are included in the casket, such as six coins to assist in navigating the River of Three Crossings – an idea somewhat similar to the Greek concept of the Styx, which the dead must cross in order to find peace. Favourite items of the deceased, such as cigarettes and sweets, are also placed in the casket. The body is normally placed with its head toward the north, called *kitamakura*, which relates to mythology regarding the way

---

27: Boret, Sébastien Penmellen. *Japanese Tree Burial: Ecology, Kinship and the Culture of Death.*

that Buddha entered nirvana. Or sometimes it is faced to the west, which is connected to what is thought of as the western realm of Amida buddha, the principal buddha in Pure Land Buddhism. Incidentally, because of the connection to death of the north direction some people avoid sleeping with their heads towards the north.

A Japanese wake is called *tsuya* (通夜 literally 'passing the night'). As in the west, funeral guests all wear black. Condolence money – usually between 3,000 to 30,000 Yen, depending on how close a relative they were – is given to the host/hostess in special black-and-silver envelopes called *bushūgibukuro* (不祝儀袋). In the funeral hall the immediate relatives are seated nearest the front, and after the Buddhist priest (called *bussō* 仏僧) chants a sutra the family place incense in an urn in front of the dead relative. Guests are given a small gift as they leave. The closest relatives sometimes keep a vigil overnight.

The *tsuya* is followed by the funeral process called *kokubetsu shiki* (告別式), which sees the burning of more incense and the chanting of more sutras. The departed gets a new Buddhist name – *kaimyō* (戒名) – the kanji for which often have ancient and esoteric meanings. The purpose of this is to prevent the return of the deceased if their name is called. A more mundane factor concerns the length of the *kaimyo*, which can depend on how large a 'donation' the family makes to the temple – a practice that some consider rather exploitative. The casket is sealed and then transported to the crematorium where the family witnesses the moving of the body into the cremation chamber.

Afterwards, the relatives pick the bones out of the ashes and transfer them to the urn using large chopsticks. Occasionally, it's necessary for two relatives to hold a bone at the same time. Known as *kotsuage* (骨揚げ), this is the only situation in which it is appropriate for two people to hold the same item at the same time with chopsticks. This is why a Japanese person may frown when a foreigner tries to pass them some food using their chopsticks. Something to be avoided!

A grave in Japan is usually a family grave called a *haka* (墓). A *haka* will normally consist of a stone monument, a place for flowers, incense and water in front of the monument and a chamber beneath for the ashes. The date on which the *haka* is established is often noted along with the names of the deceased (though this is not always the case). The name of a living spouse may be seen in red next to the dead spouse's, and when they pass too on the red is removed. We may search for symbolism in this but it seems to be done basically for the sake of prudence, to save money by engraving the two names at the same time. Some graves also have a box for business cards so you can let the main caretaker know that you were kind enough to pay a visit.

A more recent practice (or a revival of an older one perhaps) is that of tree-burials called *jumokusō* (樹木葬), created by a Zen Buddhist monk. In this, forests serve as cemeteries, with the burial of each person's ashes marked by a tree. Part of the appeal of tree-burial is that it is eco-friendly. In purchasing a tree and space in the forest, families are supporting the maintenance of Japan's woodlands and reintroducing species which may have died out in the area.[28]

A more informal, yet moving example of how the Japanese commemorate the dead are the roadside markers where a loved one has been killed in a road accident. These markers, called *osonae* (お供え offerings), sometimes develop into miniature gardens as the mourning relatives build it up into a shrine. They also function as a symbolic criticism of the poor

28: Boret, Sébastien Penmellen. *Japanese Tree Burial: Ecology, Kinship and the Culture of Death.*

A moving way to mark a tragedy, these roadside graves with flowers, beer cans, and personal items can be seen at places where a person has been killed in a road accident.

road and pavement system in Japan which, sadly, leaves a lot to be desired – another relatively unknown aspect of the country. Bicycle lanes are normally either far too narrow or simply non-existent, while cars still dominate in most cities in Japan; a situation which will have to be changed sometime, in a world more and more focused on environmental sustainability.

James Shields neatly surmises the nature of magical thinking in Japan, particularly in relation to how people cope with such phenomena as earthquakes: '…the notion that everything is always already in a higher or transformed state—the effective collapsing of sacred and profane, secular and religious—allows practice to be understood as an expression of connectedness rather than a means to connectedness.'[29] Earlier I mentioned Payne's observation that Mount Fuji is not simply a symbol of something magical, but is magical in and of itself. If, for example, the stone in your garden is already in a higher state, then the magical is already close by – it's all around us. By that logic, the distinction between sacred and profane isn't all that clear-cut or meaningful; it isn't necessary to think of object X as secular and object Y as religious. The knife you cut your bread with is as magical and meaningful an object as a cross worn round the neck.

Shields also happens to cite Richard Payne, who has argued for a new approach to the study of ritual culture in Japan, free from the bonds of Western religious studies and the assumption that ritual derives from doctrine. This is an important point, it seems to me. Doctrine refers to a belief or set of beliefs, principles or philosophical positions prescribed, for example, by a Church or political party. In Japan the ties between ritual and specific doctrine appear less tightly bound.

29: Shields, James Mark. "Beyond Belief: Japanese Approaches to the Meaning of Religion." *Studies in Religion*

OMIKUJI (おみくじ) AND OTHER FORTUNE CHARMS

There are various types of Japanese good luck charms, known as *omamori* (お守り) or *omikuji* (おみくじ), found in Buddhist temples and Shinto shrines. Most seem to have connections to ancient Chinese fortune telling. A numbered strip of bamboo is drawn at random from a cylindrical container with a small hole in one end. Then, for a nominal charge of about 100 Yen, the strip is exchanged for an *omikuji*. The good luck *omikuji* are normally taken home and treasured while bad luck *omikuji* are left tied to a tree. Tens of millions of Japanese purchase these charms every year. While some would say that very few actually believe in the specific fortune given, the practice continues – an indication that it still has social value in helping people to feel they are connecting to some magical energy, a thing which is pleasing in itself. There are omamori for many situations, including:

> **Success Talisman** (*yakuyoke* 厄除け)
> **Ward Away Evil Amulet** (also called *yakuyoke* 厄除け)
> **Money Talisman** (*shōbai hanjō* 商売繁盛)
> **Education & Learning Talisman** (*gakugyō jōju* 学業成就)
> **Traffic Safety Amulet** (*kōtsū anzen* 交通安全)
> **Love Talisman** (*enmusubi* 縁結び)
> **Luck-boosting Talisman** (*kaiun* 開運)
> **Happiness Amulet** (*shiawase* 幸せ)[30]

From listing these charms, we can see not just how many of them there are, but also the range of everyday aspects they cover, from education to love

---

30: Jacobsen, Natalie. "Japanese Lucky Charms: A Guide to Omamori." *Tokyo Weekender*.

'What does yours say?' A young couple take part, like tens of millions of others, in the fun magical activity of getting a fortune charm.

and relationships to travelling. An excellent example of mundane magic and practice in action.

Omikuji are sometimes used when performing magic to mean something akin to the term 'abracadabra'. But hold on – what is the meaning and origin of 'abracadabra' in the first place? This is another example of something commonplace in magic that very few know the origin or symbolic meaning of. While the exact origin of 'abracadabra' in common parlance is not clear, it's believed that its first written occurrence is in the second century works of Serenus Sammonicus, a doctor to the then-Roman Emperor Caracalla. It is thought by some to derive from to Hebrew meaning 'I will create as I speak' or the Aramaic meaning 'I create like the word', though again, no definitive proof has been found for either.

According to Sammonicus in his book *De Medicina Praecepta Saluberrima* the magical phrase was useful when worn on an amulet to ease the suffering of malaria, the letter representing it being repeated to form a triangle design. It was also spoken as an incantation to protect against various diseases. The Gnostics used it in magic to ask for the aid of 'good' spirits that guarded against misfortune. In this way, its usage appears very similar to the way in which the Japanese use *omikuji* charms.

Another common practice is to place a different sort of protective charm called *omajinai* (お呪い) at key points around your house, particularly at doors and windows. Nowadays, these can come in handy sticker format for ease of application. The previous resident of the house I now live in put several small golden stickers on certain entrance points. These all have a brown pyramid-like image on them; the pyramid is made of wave-like lines and looks very pleasing. There are two on each part of the window right next to where I'm typing this: one at the bottom and another at the top of each corner, and a further four in the middle where the two sections of the sliding window part, making a total of six stickers. For extra protection they also put a sticker at the bottom, fixed section of the window frame. So, I have ten protective *omajinai* stickers protecting me as I write this.

But again, this begs the question: does this magic work? How could little mass-produced stickers protect us against evil influences? Surely they don't work – not really? To revisit the earlier quote from Alan Moore, if gods exist in our minds, then so too might these stickers draw their efficacy from the same source. Perhaps that's why we feel they protect us. They have a kind of placebo effect, producing positive change even though they have no 'active ingredients' themselves. If we end up feeling more protected, calm, safe and relaxed as a result of having them there, we can say that the magic has indeed worked.

Fortune tellers (*uranaishi* 占い師) are another popular tradition in Japan, regularly consulted regarding important events or decisions. Just after I married a Japanese woman, we were taken to see an old lady to assess my aura and the chances of our marriage being successful. This took place at her house, and reminded me of the scene in the Woody Allen movie *Broadway Danny Rose*: a superstitious character played by Mia Farrow goes to see an old Italian magic lady, sitting up in her bed at home.

The fortune teller concluded that I was a good man but that there may be trouble ahead in the marriage. I smiled at the compliment and we all laughed, perhaps slightly nervously, at the possibility. We got divorced four years later, though hopefully I'm still – mostly – a good man.

HANAMI (花見) SPRING RITUAL

Hanami (花見 flower viewing) is the traditional Japanese custom of enjoying the transient beauty of flowers (*hana* 花), mostly those of the cherry tree (*sakura* 桜). This is perhaps one of the best-known Japanese festivals to the rest of the world, and is often imitated. In late March or early April, a vast amount of people attend *hanami* events in public parks, normally in small groups. Food and drink are shared, and the beautiful *sakura* petals are admired as they gently fall around the people sitting on mats. The mats in question have become standardised – a thick blue sheet which most people now use.

Especially beautiful is the *hanami* at night, which is called *yozakura* (夜桜), with the blue mats being placed near park lights or special lanterns brought by the groups themselves. In some places, such as Ueno Park in Tokyo, temporary paper lanterns are hung up around this time. In Okinawa, lovely-looking electric lanterns are hung in the trees, such as those ascending Mt. Yae near Motobu Town. The scene is a warm and charming one, with people jovially, but still civilly, enjoying a drink with family or work colleagues. It's rare to see any drunkenness, fighting or even loud partying.

Japan has a very low level of public violence, and drunken fights on the weekends are extremely rare. Violent crime rates in general are but a tiny fraction of what they are in the USA. *Hanami* is a prime example of this with the way in which it serves to bring social groups together. And since it happens around the time of the new school and work year, it is also used to cement new bonds.

Hanami festival is very old, dating at least as far back as its mention in the Heian era (794-1185) novel, *The Tale of Genji*. Originally it was associated with *ume* (梅 plum blossoms), but later became more focused on sakura blossoms. It was also used, in part, to magically divine that year's

The wonderful community festival of *Hanami* is going strong despite its ancient roots.

harvest, so its initial purpose seems to lie partly in making offerings of food and drink to the gods of the trees in exchange for a good harvest. The later focus of poems to the sakura centred around the symbolic power of the flowers themselves, however, as metaphors for the fleeting beauty of life.

It's surprising how non-commercial this festival is. There is no big corporate takeover here, no sponsors, no Coca-Ccola banners to be seen – just a mass movement of small groups, families and individual company outings. In a world increasingly dominated by corporate advertising, the almost entirely corporate-free character of *hanami* is notable and pleasing. Some even see it as an anarchistic: local groups coming together voluntarily, with no profit involved, in free public areas (the commons) for the sake of enjoying and celebrating community and the beauty of nature. Magical anarchism.

Now we come to one of my favourite festivals in Japan: *undōkai* (運動会 school sports day). The Japanese school sports system started in the 1870s, an example of the Western influence that characterized the Meiji era. According to *Undōkai to Nihon Kindai* ('Sports Day and Modern Japan') by professor Shunya Yoshimi of the University of Tokyo, the first such event took place in 1874 at the Imperial Naval College at the suggestion of an admiral of the British Royal Navy, Archibald L. Douglas. At that time, the association between sport and the military was strong in the UK; so goes the famous saying popularly attributed to the Duke of Wellington: 'The battle of Waterloo was won on the playing fields of Eton.' It was thought that sports were an cffcctive way of building discipline, competitive spirit and – somewhat paradoxically – good team co-operation. Such sports events were also held at Sapporo Agricultural College and at what was to become the University of Tokyo. They were then introduced to high schools, junior high and elementary schools (gymnastics was made compulsory in elementary schools).

While the martial origin of the *undōkai* is clear, we should note that the *undōkai* days started long before the 1930s fascist form of militarism and there is no mention at all now (and not for more than 60 years) of any active militarism at *undokai* events. It's true that some old songs are played which older generations might associate with nationalism, but the connection is not made specifically apparent to the young children involved; in all likelihood,

51

most of them have little to no idea of the association. These *undōkai* festivals now function as important yearly events, bringing people together in a way which fosters community spirit of the type that Durkeim thought so important. In this way, they're much like *Obon* dances or celebrating the return of spring with workmates at *hanami* festivals – events which can be seen as something like magical expression and a reaffirmation of community.

The events themselves normally occur in the autumn (September/October) or in the spring (May/June). October 10th is a popular date because of the association with the opening ceremony of the 1964 Tokyo Olympics. A lot of preparation goes into *undokai* festivals on the part of the teachers, kids and even some parents. During the events the principal will normally make a speech and various games will be played. Some are more serious races while other activities are silly and fun, such as the tug of war, relay races for different age groups, groups of kids forming pyramids, and the *pan kui kyōsō* (パン食い競 donut on a string game). There is also *tamaire* (玉入れ), a game played by a red team and a white team, the object of which is to get as many small beanbags as possible into a basket on top of a tall pole; *kibasen*

Go, go, go! School sports day is another festival that brings people together every year.

(騎馬戦), a cavalry game played in teams of four (three team members hold a fourth atop them as a rider who then tries to steal the headbands or caps from other teams); and finally, one that always raises a lot of laughter, *ōdama korogashi* (大玉転がし), a ball-rolling race using a giant ball that's difficult to control.

Sometimes the parents also have a race or take part in silly games. I took part in the adult tug of war (*tsunahiki* 綱引き) several times and always came away with rope burns on my arms, but it's good fun. During lunch break there is a mass (but rather tidy and well-arranged) picnic around the playing fields. The children normally eat with their families, which often means three generations huddled together on the infamous blue mats again: kids, parents and grandparents.

The glory of painting the sky on *hanabi* fireworks night.

HANABI (花火) FIREWORKS

While firework displays are often held to mark the liminal events of New Year in other parts of the world, this is not common in Japan. They are, however, very popular in the summer; known as *hanabi* (花火 literally 'flowers of fire'), they are a tradition that goes back centuries. They were originally used to ward off evil spirits, and are now staple fixtures in July and August during what is, as should be clear by now, an event-filled yearly schedule of magical festivals in Japan.

Hanabi fireworks are, of course, especially popular with children, but also with people in general. Crowds gather in special firework-viewing parks or at street shops along roads with good views to watch them. It's common to wear light *yukata* clothes and for special food stalls to be set up on these occasions. In some places, special entertainment lights up the night too. The most popular viewing spots sometimes have to be booked in advance, otherwise you have to arrive very early to claim your place. These displays often take place over parks, castles or rivers; one such is Tokyo's Sumida River Fireworks where the hanabi are launched from barges placed at strategic points along the Sumida River, creating a beautiful long flow of interconnected explosions. The composer Benjamin Britten was inspired by the Sumida River and the Noh play of the same name to write his 1964 piece *Curlew River*.

The most common shape for the fireworks to take are star mines, but hearts, smiley faces and cartoon characters also feature, and the displays can last for an hour or two, or be divided into shorter segments. There is also normally a dramatic grande finale to close off the display. There are even hanabi competitions. The Ōmagari National Fireworks Competition is a special event taking place along the Marukogawa River in Akita Prefecture, in which teams battle to outshine or 'outburst' each other. .

Besides the bigger fireworks there is, of course, the children's favourite too: handheld sparklers, called *senkō hanabi* (線香花火). These are popular in numerous countries now. They originated in Edo-era Japan, and like many of the everyday magical things we are considering in this book, they have a deeper meaning beyond that of simply having fun: the movement of the *senkō hanabi* is sometimes thought to be able to hypnotize watchers into a calm, reflective silence. The fleeting beauty of the light is an example of the *wabi-sabi* (侘寂) aesthetic of Japan with its awareness of the ephemeral nature of existence. The short-lived beauty of the sparkler evokes what is called *mono no aware* (物の哀れ, empathy toward things or sensitivity to ephemera) – a central part of what this book refers to as 'the spirit of Japan'. This is a powerful – though everyday – demonstration of how such magical thinking and experiences can help us to deepen our understanding both of

With sparklers we can all feel like we have a magic wand, for a short time anyway.

ourselves and the world around us. Not bad for a sparkler that costs less than a hotdog!

The idea and practice of *wabi-sabi* is particularly apt concerning the magic of physical objects, and has influenced many artists, architects, gardeners and designers. As Richard Powell notes in his book on the subject: '*Wabi-sabi* nurtures all that is authentic by acknowledging three simple realities: nothing lasts, nothing is finished, and nothing is perfect.'[31]

The concept of authenticity is not an easy one to pin down, but the three simple realities seem undeniably true of all human and physical life. Such a philosophy may seem too metaphysical to be of much use on a day-to-day basis; but the beautiful gardens and objects imbued with *wabi-sabi* help us to develop a calm appreciation of what is, of what we already have in life, rather than constantly chasing after new products and goals and money. It can be seen as a contrary way of thinking to the dominant drives of modern consumerism, capitalism and the social pressure to 'keep up with the Joneses'. The art of *kintsugi* exemplifies this: cracked pottery is filled with gold dusted lacquer which further shows, rather than hides, its age and its flaws. This is symbolic of the pain and ugliness that accumulates over a lifetime, representing the imperfections we gain; but instead of covering them up with makeup, plastic surgery or Botox, we lay them out honestly and accept them with grace and dignity. In this, *wabi-sabi* and the magic of art are reminiscent of the modern mindfulness movement – helping us to deal with the realities of existence.

Probably the most well-known examples of this are Japanese gardens, which revolve around the animistic belief that objects have spirits or magical energy. As a result, we find many elements of nature incorporated into their design: small gravel, larger stones and rocks, islands in ponds, small hills (sometimes symbolic of larger, famous places), teahouses and bridges. There are streams, fish, strolling paths, stone-lanterns, bamboo pipes and water basins; moss, flowers, trees, statues, gates and fences. The Nanzenji Temple Zen Garden in Kyoto is a particularly popular attraction which receives many visitors.

Alex Bradshaw holds a very rare position for a foreigner in Japan as the Head of Overseas Business for the Shimadzu Clan of Kagoshima. On the topic of gardens, he makes this observation: 'Passing through the

31: Powell, Richard R. *Wabi Sabi Simple.*

entrance of a garden is really intended to be akin to stepping into another world where your imagination brings the canvas of the garden to life. Most people have this totally wrong these days. They think that the gardens are places to learn about history or who built them, but they were never intended as history museums.'[32] These gardens are about magical thinking, about transformative processes in the here and now. They are not intended to be distant monuments no longer of relevance to everyday life.

In the case of other magical elements in use today, however, historical origins can actually serve to enhance our appreciation of them further. Fireworks were first introduced to Japan around 1600, possibly for Masamune Date in 1589 or for Tokugawa Ieyasu in 1613. These dates may seem surprising considering the fact that in England, the earliest recorded fireworks display took place more than 100 years before that, on Henry VII's wedding day in 1486. Surely Japan, via China, was using fireworks long before they arrived in western Europe? Especially since it's known that the Chinese had invented gunpowder by 900AD at the latest, and that fireworks displays for various rituals and festivals became a feature of the Song dynasty (960–1279).

Research by the Koloa Jodo Mission Buddhist Temple in Hawaii claims: 'One of the first documents which mentioned the usage of the fireworks was a private diary called "Kennaiki" written by Madenokōji Tokifusa (1395-1457). There was an article dated March 21, 1447 which says "After a memorial service at Shojokein Temple which is a Jōdō sect temple, some kind of arts by fire was performed and because it was so splendid like a shooting star, Tokifusa praised and gave an award to the people who seemed to be Chinese. Since there were trade ships going back and forth between Japan and Ming Dynasty during the Muromachi era (1336-1573), it is considered that fireworks were brought to Japan during this time.'[33]

On a related note, a Chinese ship with Portuguese merchants on board which came to Japan in 1543 was recorded as having guns amongst its cargo. Once again it seems odd that technology such as guns, gunpowder and cannon would only come to Japan via far-off Portugal when China itself was so near. Other historians point out that early powder cannons called *teppō* (鉄砲 iron cannon) actually probably first appeared in Japan around 1270. It's likely, however,

---

32: Bradshaw, Alex. Interview by author, October, 2020.
33: Koloa Jodo Mission. "Meaning of Hanabi – A Brief History of Fireworks in Japan."

that these were very primitive, and that the more advanced guns brought by the Portuguese 250 years later had a far wider influence in Japan. To return to the subject of fireworks, it is thought that 1582 a Portuguese missionary once put on such a display at a temple for the Christian missionaries under the protection of Lord Ōtomo Sōrin.

Whenever it was that fireworks displays started in Japan, the tradition seems to have become associated with the *Obon* celebrations discussed in Chapter 3 as part of an effort to welcome benevolent spirits and see off malign ones from the other side. The fireworks at Sumida river mentioned earlier began in 1733, the year after a famine killed many and caused great suffering for those who survived. The fireworks acted as a symbolic goodbye to the dead of the year before and as a way to lift the hearts of those still living.

In the first chapter we briefly touched upon the power in the sound of bells. This bell sound is an integral part of the magic of its ceremony – an internal, meditative noise that seems to resonate at a physical level within us. Other instances of music and sound like the drums of the *taiko* (太鼓) or the singing of the Autumn horse festival in Kumamoto can, of course, stir us to greater energy, or to dance. The bursting sound of fireworks is a key part of the experience of the show.

Wooooooshhh! (Up they go)…

Craaaacckkkk! (They burst into sound, light, existence)…

Fuuushhh... (They fall to the ground, extinguished, burnt out).

The spluttering sound as they fall away back down to earth is symbolic of things coming to an end, of the fleetingness of life. The display ends in the deep sound of silence.

That's all folks…

Earlier in the book we examined the idea that magic and science can be complimentary. Music is perhaps another good example of this. Music allows a balance of emotions and logic; in the process of playing an instrument, it is normal to learn certain formal techniques and follow patterns which have a certain mathematical order to them. There is order, there are fixed relationships between the tones, the keys, the strings and so on, and we manipulate these to express our emotions as we play, and to provoke emotions in the listener. Music is the controlled expression of emotions, the focused expression of mental and physical energy. According to the 18th century Swiss philosopher

Jean Pierre de Crousaz: '...the highest form of aesthetic judgement (bon gout) depends on an equal partnership of reason and sentiment.'[34]

The Chinese philosopher Xunzi (c. 310–c. 220 B.C.E.) was, along with Confucius and Mencius, one of the three main figures in early Confucian philosophy. Xunzi and his contemporaries considered music a very important part of ritual. He thought that the music used in rituals transformed people: mournful music caused people to feel sad, military music aroused action, seductive music encourages dissolute behaviour, etc. However: 'The task of nurturing the emotions through "external" tools such as ritual and music thus amounts to more than the shaping of emotions and desires through the rational mind... through the proper deployment of ritual (as well as music), both emotions... and form... achieve their perfected state...'[35]

Certainly music is an integral aspect of rituals and ceremonies in Japan, often in a highly formalized way, but it serves the important role of helping us mark the change from the profane to the sacred. It also helps to bond us to others taking part in the music and dance, while still providing a very personal emotional and cognitive experience. Renfrew and Morley's collection notes: '...musical activities are a remarkably effective facilitator of the desired effects of participation in ritual activities. The performance and perception of music can provide the perfect medium for carrying symbolic (including religious) associations because of its combination of having no fixed meaning ('floating intentionality') whilst having the potential to stimulate powerful emotional reactions.'[36]

In the city I live in, Kumamoto, there is a old dancing song called *Otemoyan* (おてもやん) composed by Ine Nagata, a gifted geisha musician from the late 19th century, and thought to be named after a woman called Tomo Tominaga. "Tomo" was pronounced "Temo" in the old Kumamoto accent, and the song is full of words in the local dialect. The song is often performed in the *Hinokuni Matsuri* (火の国祭) festival, which is held on the first Friday and Saturday of August every year in Kumamoto City. The city centre is blocked off from cars, and around 5,000 local people dance through the streets. This festival is symbolic of the height of summer – though not only in a theoretical sense, as Kumamoto is very hot in the summer! Singing

---

34: Crousaz in Trezise, Simon (ed). *The Cambridge Companion to French Music.*
35: Virág, Curie. *The Emotions in Early Chinese Philosophy.*
36: Renfrew, Colin and Morley, Iain (eds). *Becoming Human.*

the song during this dance connects people to an older time in the city's history, especially via the local accent in the lyrics, and helps cement good community feeling in the present day.[37]

The words of the song are rather comical, with the woman saying she is not officially married because her husband is too ugly. She flirts with other men around town and declares that she loves a man in another town.

JAPANESE LYRICS

おてもやん　あんたこの頃嫁入りしたではないかいな
嫁入りしたこつぁしたばってん　ご亭どんがグジャッペだるけん
まぁだ盃はせんだった
村役　鳶役　肝煎りどん　あん人たちのおらすけんで
あとはどうなっときゃあなろたい
川端町っつぁん　きゃぁめぐろ
春日ぼうぶらどんたちゃ　尻ひっぴゃぁて花盛り花盛り
ピーチクパーチク雲雀の子　げんばく茄子のいがいがどん

一つ山越え　も一つ山越え　あの山越えて
私しゃあんたに惚れとるばい
惚れとるばってん言われんたい
追々彼岸も近まれば　若者衆も寄らすけん
くまんどんのよじょもん詣りにゆるゆる話しもきゃぁしゅぅたい
男振りには惚れんばな
煙草入れの銀金具が　それがそもそも因縁たい
アカチャカ　ベッチャカ　チャカチャカ　チャー

37: Noren, Anders. "Journey of Otemoyan (おてもやん) and the Writer of the Song, the Most Famous Folk Song in Kumamoto." *Untapped Kumamoto.*

ENGLISH TRANSLATION

Miss Otemo
Weren't you married just recently?
As a matter of fact, I was. However,
Since my husband's face is all pockmarked,
We haven't had a proper ceremony.
Our village is replete with busybodies.
Those people will take care everything.
So, no worry.
Let's go walk around the downtown Kawabata.
Guys ripe like Kasuga pumpkins
They all try to get hold of me -I'm like a flower in full bloom.
Men chirping away like skylarks, unattractive and unfashinable,
They're just not my type.

You are mountains away from me.
I'm so in love with you
Though I can't confess it.
As the Feast of the Equinox approaches,
Many young people will gather in throngs.
At the Yojomon Pilgrimage in Kumamoto
I wish to take time and chat with you.
It wasn't your looks that charmed me.
Fate sometimes attracts us to simple things,
like the silver fittings on your cigarette case.
Dum diddle dee diddle
Diddle diddle daa.

Of course, the best-known Japanese musical ritual in the world is karaoke. Even this – an activity that is, on the face of it, a fun, recreational thing – has taken on deeper, more meaningful aspects. One area which has come into particular focus recently is how karaoke can help to release job stress and friction in workplace hierarchy. Hiroko Kimura, a music therapist in Japan, told me: 'People seem to use karaoke as a way of expressing annoyance and dissatisfaction with work that they cannot do directly to their boss'.[38] In this way, karaoke can be seen as a modern ritual which helps people cope with the stresses of work and life in general.

Mac Salman, Founder and Lead Guide of Maction Planet Bespoke Japan Tours, tellsa rather comical anecdote along these lines from when he joined a new company: 'After a few songs, someone picked the classic track "Imagine" by John Lennon. I was keen to join my colleagues in attempting to sing this famous piece of music. The first line of the lyrics is "Imagine there's no countries" but I was the only one who sang those words. Everyone else was singing "Imagine there's no Shima." Shima-san was the name of our boss.'[39]

38: Hiroko Kimura. Interview by author, March 2020.
39: Salman, Mac. "Need a break from a stressful boss? Try taking him to karaoke." *Linkedin.*

New land and buildings being cleansed of bad spirits.

LAND-CLEANSING RITUALS

When an old house is knocked down, a Shinto ritual is performed on the empty lot. It is called *jichinsai* (地鎮祭) and is conducted in preparation for starting construction on the new house or business. This type of purification rite serves several purposes: firstly, since construction causes a lot of disturbance, it is thought necessary to appease the spirits of the land, to get them 'onside' for the new project. Secondly, it helps to ensure the safety of the construction workers, and that work goes ahead according to schedule and without mishap. Lastly, to assist the future tenants or business that will occupy the cleansed land; banish the bad vibes and start afresh. Shinto priests are booked in advance to perform the ceremony under specially-erected tents. A mound of earth is made under the tent, like a mini Mount Fuji, and a solemn ceremony is carried out. The cost of this is included in the construction budget.

Roof-raising ceremonies, *jōtōsai* (上棟祭), also called *muneageshiki* (棟上げ式 roof-raising) are rituals performed during construction of a new building in the hope that it will make certain there are no problems with the new roof. This ritual is another of very long standing, thought to have been used for the Imperial Palace beginning in the mid-Heian period (ninth and tenth centuries) and fOr the Grand Shrines of Isein in the early-Kamakura period (12th century).

'The jōtōsai was not among the Shinto rites formalized in the 1875 Rules for Ritual Procedure at Shrines, so it took various forms in different regions, but today the Association of Shinto Shrines (*Jinja Honchō* 神社本庁) has established a standardized version for it in its *Shosaishiki yōkō* (諸祭式要綱 Outline of Various Ceremonies). The first of these is the rope-pulling ritual, which symbolizes the raising of the ridgepole onto the rooftop. The second is the mallet-striking ritual, wherein the ridgepole is symbolically pounded into place. The third and final ritual is that of scattering offerings, in which *mochi* (餅 rice cake) and coins are tossed to those below. After those three rituals are concluded, the ceremony finishes with a ritual bow, a ritual scattering of rice offerings, and the ascent of the kami.'[40]

If we once again consider the purpose such magic serves for those who take part, we can perhaps imagine a case in which a company or building owner decided not to have a *jichinsai* ceremony. Imagine the look of horror on the face of the owner's grandmother when she discovers this. 'That will bring bad luck on your new house. Oh, no, I won't go in there. No way.' Or if the construction workers hear there will be no such ritual, they might react something like this: 'What? Oh, I am not happy with that. My friend worked on a house with no *jichinsai* ceremony and you know what happened to him? He fell off the roof on the first day. Broke his leg!' It might even result in a 'magical strike' with the workers refusing to enter the site.

But imagine if all that was swept aside and the house was built. It's quite possible that every misfortune that happened to come along would be put down to bad spirits not being happy with the new building. If it were a block of rental apartments, the word might get round that it's haunted or bad luck, making the properties difficult to let. If it were a business, people may think of it as unlucky to have dealings with them, and soon enough, they would close down! Of course, none of that means there are actual restless spirits causing the new building to be unlucky or causing incidents – it may be entirely in the minds of the people who interact with the 'unclean' building. But when one simple ceremony dispels all that for a moderate cost, why not have it?

However, the practice of clearing away greenery for the sake of cleansing has become a negative side-effect of the ceremony. In an age when green issues have become so key, the practice of killing all the trees and plant life in such plots is bad for the environment and it would be good to see this addressed. A surprising thing about Japan, given that its people are said to have a deep love and respect for nature, is that there appears to be little thought given to basic environmental issues. When houses are demolished, there is a bad habit here of cutting down all the trees in the former garden, leaving the ground 90-100% cleared, ready for new construction. This seems to happen as a matter of course in almost all cases, even when the trees in the

---

40: Kokugakuin University. Encyclopedia of Shinto. "Jōtōsai."

garden are very old or when there seems little need to fell them. The usual practice is to build a new house or apartment blocks with only one or two trees on the plot — or in many cases, none at all. This seems to fly in the face of good environmental practice, and to display a worrying lack of concern for maintaining the physical culture and beauty of Japan's landscape.[41]

It seems apt, at this point, to once again mention the importance of animism in Japan. Animist belief holds that all things have a spirit or a consciousness. The 2019 collection of essays *Spirits and Animism in Contemporary Japan* looks at how animism is not simply a defunct, ancient practice but something which continues to have an effect on everyday life in Japan even now, and particularly the ways in which: '…manga, anime, TV shows, literature, and art works deal with spirits, ghosts, or with an invisible dimension of reality.'[42]

We have already considered various examples of 'animism in action' over the course of previous chapters, such as the blessing of cars and houses and how my son's Japanese grandmother did not want me to

41: Wilson, Sean Michael. "With every new construction in Japan, fewer trees." *The Japan Times*.
42: Rambelli, Fabio (ed). *Spirits and Animism in Contemporary Japan*.

Sadly, old houses are being knocked down and gardens destroyed at an alarming rate.

bring an old stone into the house. The 2019 essay collection also attempts to trace the cultural genealogies of these beliefs as well as the underlying intellectual and religious assumptions we might see there. Perhaps my son's granny thinks the stone is alive, that it has its own spirit or energy — that it's magical. It may not wish to be brought into a new setting; at least not without a respectful ritual asking its permission or cleansing it of past energy. It may bring negative spirits in and pollute the house. Better to leave it where it is.

Manga and anime are modern mediums in which the tenets of animism may frequently be seen. Miyazaki Hayao of Studio Ghibli expressed this eloquently:

"The major characteristic of Studio Ghibli – not just myself – is the way we depict nature. We don't subordinate the natural setting to the characters. Our way of thinking is that nature exists and human beings exist within it. ... That is because we feel that the world is beautiful. Human relationships are not the only thing that is interesting. We think that weather, time, rays of light, plants, water, and wind – what makes up the landscape – are all beautiful. That is why we make efforts to incorporate them as much as possible in our work."[43]

Miyazaki's focus on a magical relationship with nature serves to reconnect modern audiences to this idea. The anime *Weathering with You*, already mentioned previously, is another recent example which focuses on the importance of climate and nature. Given this emphasis on respect for the environment, and the growing awareness of the need to protect it that we see in these manga and anime, it strikes me as odd that trees in private gardens are not shown the respect due to something which has a spirit and is so important to the ecosystem.

Or maybe the people ordering the trees' destruction, and the people who carry it out, feel regret at the deaths of these living things but push it to the back of their minds. By chance, a gardener was pruning trees in the garden opposite me and I put this question to him (a nice man; he gave me a cutting from a mulberry tree and I planted it in my own garden). After getting past the surprise of a foreigner suddenly asking him about this he said: 'This pruning is ok, it helps the trees grow. But I feel a little sad when I

43: Yoneyama, Shoko, "Rethinking Human-Nature Relationships in the Time of Coronavirus: Postmodern Animism in Films by Miyazaki Hayao & Shinkai Makoto." *Asia Pacific Journal.*

have to cut down a tree completely. But it's part of my job. What can I do?'
We can hardly criticise such people. He has bills to pay. Economic concerns
overpower the spiritual, and we all grow poorer.

Still, it seems clear that the *jichinsai* magical ritual, and the practice
of clearing away all the greenery that goes with it, could be adjusted so that
it no long requires the removal of all trees from a plot. Or, if the clearing
is thought to be absolutely necessary for the sake of cleansing, perhaps the
replanting of trees after the ritual to a minimum of 25% of the number that
was there before would suffice. This would strike a good balance between
respecting nature and maintaining the central intent of the *jichinsai* ritual —
just in a more environmentally friendly fashion.

Fortunately, there are signs that such thinking may be on the rise. In
her consideration of anime's involvement in the of rethinking human-nature
relationships, Yoneyama has this to say: 'I argue that what I call 'postmodern
animism' emerged as a grassroots response to the socio-ecological disaster
in Minamata... Postmodern animism represents new knowledge that arose
from the fusion of critiques of modernity and the intangible cultural heritage
of grassroots Japan. It represents a philosophy of the life-world, where nature
is seen as a manifestation of a dynamic life force in which all forms of life
are interconnected. It is animism imbued with modernity while deliberately
keeping the core components of animism: i.e. nature and spirituality.'

The reference to Minamata pertains to a man-made disaster which
came to light in the 1950s in Kumamoto, the prefecture I now live in.
Methylmercury from a factory there was funneled out into the sea, causing
mercury poisoning in the fish which in turn found its way into the bodies
of locals who ate the fish. Widespread, debilitating health conditions were
the result, and thousands of local people were affected. News of the disaster
spread, and a campaign to secure compensation developed into a wider
critique of pollution caused by irresponsible capitalist corporations and the
government's backing of them. Yoneyama notes that that campaign has had
a demonstrably positive influence on how we think of our relationship with
nature – the ways in which we conduct our activities to accord it greater
respect, and our recognition of our magical connection with it. Postmodernism
animism, indeed.

Thankfully, shrines and temples are protected and maintained.

RITUALS AT SHRINES
AND TEMPLES

The particulars of visiting a Shinto shrine are among the best-known examples of Japanese magic, since these are often popular destinations with tourists. Practices such as the cleansing rituals carried out upon entering the holy magical ground of the shrine, and the process of clapping and bowing when making an offering or praying, are likely to be some of the most widely recognised.

When you go into a shrine or temple there is normally a little roofed hut to the side called a *chōzuya* or *temizuya* (both written as 手水舎). In smaller temples it's sometimes just a simple enclosure with no roof. Here you will find a washbasin for ritual purification, *kiyomeru* (清める, which is also sometimes used for tea ceremonies. The original preference (which persists today) for the contents of the washbasin was water from a natural spring; for example, at the *Ise Jingū* (伊勢神宮 Ise Grand Shrine) in Mie Prefecture, people cleanse themselves with water from the Isuzu River. The washbasins are called *tsukubai* (蹲踞), which comes from the verb *tsukubau* meaning to crouch or to bow down in an act of humility during the ritual.

Visitors wash their hands and rinse their mouths in what is essentially a simplified version of *misogi* (禊). *Misogi* is a washing purification ritual still practiced by a small number of devoted people which involves cleansing the whole body—for example, the misogi performed at night under a waterfall at Tsubaki Grand Shrine (*Tsubaki Ōkamiyashiro* 椿大神社), also in Mie Prefecture, which is said to be one of the oldest Shinto shrines in Japan, dating back to 3 BC).

The steps of the cleansing process are as follows:

1. Take one of the ladles from on top of the water basin. Using your right hand to hold the ladle, fill it with fresh water from the basin. One cupful of water should be enough for the whole ritual.

2. With your hands away from the basin so the water does not drip back in, pour the water gently over your left hand. Then, holding the ladle in your left hand, pour water over your right.

3. Take some of the water into your mouth. This is usually done by pouring some water into your cupped hand, normally the left – your mouth should not touch the ladle itself. Rinse your mouth a bit, then spit the water onto the rocks, again making sure not to spit any into the basin.

4. Lastly, hold the ladle upright so the water flows down the handle – this will clean it. If there is any water left, empty that out onto the rocks and finally set the ladle back on its resting place with the cup downwards.

The ritual of cleansing ourselves before entering holy ground.

When you are inside the main shrine you can go up to a central room called a *haiden* (拝殿) which is sometimes situated some distance away in the back of the grounds. There may be a queue so stand patiently in line. When it's your turn, climb the steps and follow this procedure:

1. Bow to the shrine, and then gently throw some money (it doesn't matter how much) into the medium-sized wooden box in front of you, called a *saisen-bako* (賽銭箱). The 5 Yen coin, pronounced *go en*, is a homophone of the word for good luck (*goen* ご縁) and is therefore thought best for offerings. But it seems to me that 100 Yen is more common now, since 5 Yen is very little money. 10 Yen is avoided as it is considered unlucky.

2. Sometimes there is a big shaker-type bell on a thick rope – give this a yank to attract the attention of the gods and purify the space.

3. Now comes the *ni rei, ni hakushu, ichirei* (二礼二拍手一礼) process:

4. *Ni rei*: deeply bow twice.

5. *Ni hakushu*: softly clap your hands twice. Hands should be raised to about chest level and opened to roughly shoulder-width apart before you clap. When you bring your hands together, the right hand should sit slightly below your left, as the left hand represents the gods while the right hand represents you.

6. *Ichi rei*: make another deep bow, once, to end the process.

A common question among foreign visitors is: 'what is the difference between a shrine and a temple?' The simple distinction is that shrines (*jinja* 神社) are Shintoist and temples (*tera* 寺) are Buddhist. But how to tell them apart? One indication is what form the guardians at the entrance take. Buddhist temples have statues of *Niō* (仁王, tough-looking, muscular demon guardians of the Buddha) stand guard on either side. Shrines, on the other hand, often have statues of lion-dogs called *komainu* (狛犬), though these can sometimes look more like dragons or foxes. They come in pairs on either side of the shrine entrance, or sometimes inside the shrine itself.

Confusingly, however, these lion-dog guardians seem to be derived from Indian Buddhist practices, and in the past many temples also had them. In certain cases, some still do, such as the ones that can be seen at Tōji Temple in Kyoto. The fact that these aspects are found in both temples and shrines is thought to be because grounds were shared in the past, though this rarely happens now. It's also believed that early Buddhist practitioners drew upon some of the earlier Shinto characters and symbols in the process of spreading their religion in Japan. It's often noted that *komainu* look very similar to Chinese guardian lions, the latter of which originated during the Tang dynasty via the influence of Indian symbolism wherein lions were seen as a symbol of strength.

The magical significance of these *komainu* is that they are meant to ward off evil spirits (funny how evil spirits seem to be so easily frightened!). If you look closely when visiting a shrine you will notice that it is customary for one of the lion-dogs to have an open mouth while the mouth of the other is closed. The open-mouthed lion-dog is pronouncing the first letter of the Sanskrit alphabet, 'a', and the close-mouthed one is pronouncing the last letter, 'u'. Put together they form the sound 'aum', which is a magical sound in Hinduism and Buddhism meaning the name of god or the sound of the vibration of the universe.[44]

When approaching a shrine you will pass through a large gate called *torii* (鳥居, literally bird abode). These may stand right at the entrance of the shrine or be set some distance away from it. You may not even notice the first gate as they can be large structures far above head height and right at the end of the street. Sometimes there are two or even three different *torii* as you get closer to the centre of the shrine. Normally made of wood or stone, they can be painted vermillion with a black upper part or can be left unpainted altogether. When approaching the grounds of a shrine the first thing to do is to bow your head just before the entrance *torii*. Occasionally you see Japanese people stopping to do this when they are simply walking past, even if they are not going in.

These *torii* gates have been erected in Japan since at least the mid-Heian period (794-1185); we know this because one is mentioned in a text

---

44: Traditional Kyoto. "Lions – Komainu."

written in 922. The oldest stone *torii* still standing is from the 12th century, at the Hachiman Shrine in Yamagata prefecture. To yet further confuse the difference between shrines and temples, these gates are also probably derived from Indian Buddhist practices and in the past many temples also had them. There is one in Ōsaka's Shitennōji temple, which, founded in 593, is the oldest state-built Buddhist temple in the world. These gates act as liminal markers, presiding over the change from mundane to magical ground.

Victor Turner was a central figure in promoting the importance of liminality, a concept which was also used by the French folklorist Arnold van Gennep earlier in the 20th century: 'It involves the second of three phases involved in rites of passage: separation, in which one behaves as though detached from one's group; limen in which one traverses a realm that has few or none of the familiarities of past experience; and finally, aggregation, in which one completes the passage and returns to mundane life within the social group.'[45]

So, liminality is a state in which normal boundaries and patterns are open to change; it is a state of moments both in and out of time, both inside and outside of social structure. Karaoke parties are sometimes places in which those who are 'subordinate' in the workplace may express criticism of their 'superiors' in ways that they otherwise could not. Turner talks of the importance of liminal opportunities to the weak in society as times when they can feel outside the dominating hierarchy, and can feel a greater potential than they normally do when under the heel of a boss or manager. He seemed to see liminality as the intermittent return to the *communitas* of connection – something which the tight hierarchy of ordinary society divides us from – and the 'periodical reclassification of reality and man's relationship to society, nature and culture.'[46]

William Reed, an Aikido 8th-dan, Shodo 10th-dan and Professor at Yamanashi Gakuin University International College of Liberal Arts, reminds us of a basic underlying aspect of Japanese magic which can be seen as a good example of liminality: 'To understand Japanese rituals of all kinds it

---

45: Turner, Victor, and Yamaguchi Masao (eds). *Misetnono no jirtruigaku* 見世物の人類学 *Spectacle—An Anthropological Inquiry.*
46: Turner, Victor. *The Ritual Process: Structure and Anti-Structure.*

is necessary to define the concept of *kekkai* (結界) the fixing of spiritual boundaries. Every shrine, every temple, every home has an inner and outer sanctum, separated by a gate, a door, or a rope. This is also expressed in the line drawn by placing a folding fan on the tatami in a Tea Ceremony, or by bowing to your sword before placing it in your sash. This line is either not to be crossed, or to be crossed by people who have purified themselves in some form of ritual. The simplest of these is the bow, often proceeded by the pressing together of hands (*gashou*) or clapping of hands (*kashiwade*) often seen at Shinto Shrines. Whatever the spiritual barrier, you don't barge across it without humbly announcing your presence. The purpose of such rituals is to acknowledge the spirit of a person or place, and thereby achieve harmony with it.'[47]

Mikkyō (密教 literally 'secret teachings') is a form of esoteric Tantric Buddhism that developed in China and India. It came over to Japan in the sixth century and was a marked influence on Shingon Buddhism. The Japanese word *shingon* (真言) is a version of the Chinese word *zhēnyán* (真言) which is thought to derive from the Sanskrit word mantra (a mantra being a magical sound, symbol or word). As Fabio Rambelli notes: 'An understanding of this paradigm is…essential for the study not only of medieval Japanese religiosity and culture but also of the esoteric ceremonies, magic rituals, and traditional divination still performed in contemporary Japan.'[48] It would seem that the symbolism behind many of the magical observances which are put into practice today has its origins in the mysticism, magic and healing focus of these ancient SOBU.

Take, for example, the hand-clapping aspect mentioned previously. This is something observed in many facets of Japanese life, not just shrines. Clapping your hands in this way is called *tejime* (手締め): a ceremonial custom of rhythmic clapping, done in unison with others in a group, and usually accompanied by a loud shout. The sound of the clapping, the shout and the physical feeling on the hands all combine, reinforcing the group's

47: Reed, William. Interview by author, November 2020.
48: Rambelli, Fabio. "True Words, Silence, and the Adamantine Dance." *Japanese Journal of Religious Studies.*

collective spirit and your own feeling of involvement. This simple but powerful instance of group magic is often performed at the conclusion of a special event, such as a business meeting, party or celebration to end the gathering with a sense of fulfilment and completion.

It's worth taking a moment to mention just how many shrines and temples there are in Japan. It's thought that there are between 150,000 and 190,000 of them. By comparison, there are only 16,000 Christian churches in England (though more across the UK in general).

Santa in Shinjuku? Several western ceremonies are now popular in Japan.

RECENT FOREIGN
FESTIVALS IN JAPAN

Let's turn to look now at the more recent festivals that have come to Japan from Western countries. The most notable of these is, of course, Christmas. Oddly, Japan does a lot of preparing for Christmas – but then on December 25th, no actual Christmas. For most people it's still a working day, and for most students still a study day. Yet, as I say, there is a lot of preparation. There are advent calendars, chocolate snowmen and decorations for sale, pizza delivery men dress as Santa, trees and lights are common, 'Merry Christmas' signs appear in shops, 'Jingle Bells' echoes through the mall… but on Christmas Day itself, nothing. Not a sausage - and certainly not a satsuma in a sock, as is common in the UK. And though it is becoming increasingly common for children to be given some small present on Christmas Day, the holiday itself is still largely a non-event.

Interestingly, the satsuma orange is not called a satsuma in Japan, and people react with surprise when I tell them that this is what we call it in the UK. Satsuma is a province of southern Japan. This is my personal theory as to why British people started to call the small orange by the same name: during the short Anglo-Satsuma War (薩英戦争 *Satsuei sensō*, 15th–17th August 1863) the Satsuma Clan and the British armed forces developed a respect for each other. In fact, after the war ended, the Satsuma Clan added a military band to their number because they were impressed by that of the British Navy. I imagine a scene in which the Japanese and the British exchanged gifts to seal the new friendship, and among them was the little mikan orange. With the Japanese not speaking much English and the British speaking almost no Japanese, I think it's likely that the sailors started to call the oranges 'satsuma' in reference to the place they received them from. Easy to imagine a sailor back home in, say, Portsmouth, telling his friend:

'Oh, and we got some lovely oranges in Satsuma, little soft ones.'

'Sat-what, mate?'

'Sat-su-ma. Satsuma oranges. Here, try one.'

And the name stuck. Of course, that might be totally wrong, but it's a nice story all the same.

Another festival that has become very common is Halloween, which, annoyingly for a Scot like me, almost all Japanese seem to think comes from the USA. I wrote an article for the local newspaper here in Kumamoto explaining that it actually originated in Scotland and Ireland as a Celtic magic festival more than 1,500 years before the USA declared independence. Japanese people are particularly surprised to discover that a common school sports game which involves trying catch a donut or apple held aloft on a string with only your teeth (called *pan kui kyōsō* パン食い競争 in Japan) is played in Scotland and Ireland at Halloween and has been for hundreds of years. There is a painting from 1832 (*Snap-Apple Night* by Daniel Maclise) showing a Halloween party in Blarney, Ireland, in which the adults are doing just that. The children in the painting are having fun trying to catch apples floating in a big barrel of water with their teeth – apple bobbing, or 'dooking' as it's called in Scotland.

Jesse LeFebvre's work examines another Western ritual that has become quite common in Japan: Christian style wedding ceremonies. While he initially acknowledges that the Japanese are seen as mostly non-religious, he goes on to note: '… these same individuals do also continue to engage in behaviors that might otherwise still be considered religious. Despite the prevalence of non-religiousness among the members of contemporary Japanese society there exist very few explorations into how non-religiousness functions "on the ground" as a part of people's lives or how to treat religious acts when these acts are undertaken by nonreligious individuals.'[49]

In order to facilitate this trend for Christian-style weddings, mock churches have been built based on British or European churches of the 17th century, and foreign residents are employed to wear a priest's robe and go through the motions of the ceremony. I know a few foreigners here who do this as a weekend job. I suppose there are some Christians who would

---

49: LeFebvre, Jesse. "Christian Wedding Ceremonies—'Nonreligiousness' in Contemporary Japan." *Japanese Journal of Religious Studies.*

take offence at this, and might consider it a type of cultural appropriation. However, LeFebvre mentions that research shows Japanese people seem to think of these semi-religious services as being like any other service – something that anyone can have access to, regardless of their faith or lack thereof.

LeFebvre believes the concept that the Japanese are not religious to be a way of relieving the cognitive burden of dealing with the perceived strangeness of the magical practices in Japan. Better to put it all into a nice easy box, separate from our 'normal' religious practices. Perhaps this also helps us escape the need to consider how odd our own religion may seem to others. So: 'Given this association with normalcy, "non-religiousness" is a rejection of religious associations and practices deemed unhealthy, strange, or foreign... "nonreligion" is better understood as the religious outlook of the average Japanese person who often engages in religious activity effectively and vicariously.'[50]

One important Western festival which has not caught on in Japan is Easter. It's very difficult to find the big chocolate Easter eggs that I'm familiar with from my childhood, which is a pity, as I would like to give my son such an Easter egg each year. Instead he has to make do with a packet of little chocolate eggs. Poor wee laddie! Why has this festival not taken off in Japan as much as Christmas and Halloween? It would seem as if there is plenty of visual appeal for children in the rabbits and eggs that companies could make commercial use of (I don't count companies use of such things as 'genuine', since they, of course, don't care at all about the meaningful content of any festivals, only the money it brings in). Egg-rolling activities are just the kind of festive fun that the Japanese like, too, and which schools often engage in. It's possible that Easter's being in April puts it too close to the *hanami* festivals, and that there wasn't room for another festival to develop around that time. However, Halloween takes place only 15 days before another major children's festival in Japan, the 7-5-3 Festival (七五三 *Shichi Go San*), so perhaps it's simply that Easter wasn't meant to be.

The 7-5-3 festival happens – you guessed it – when children reach three, five, and seven years of age. It is an especially cute event as the kids are dressed up in their Sunday best, with pretty mini versions of Japanese

---

50: *Ibid.* LeFebvre

kimono (着物) for the girls and *hakama* (袴) for the boys. So adorable! My own son had his five-year-old celebration in a little Scottish kilt, with me next to him in my adult kilt (of the Gunn clan, from which the Wilson name derives).

The 7-5-3 festival is rooted in a magical belief of East Asian numerology that children of certain ages are especially prone to bad luck, giving rise to the need for a ritual of protection. It is thought to date back to the Heian period (794-1185AD). Given that a high percentage of children died during childbirth at that time, it was probably also a celebration of a child reaching three, five, and seven years of age, as well as drawing on magical sources to help them survive longer still. It is estimated that as many as half of all children failed to reach adulthood. A study by Anthony Volk and Jeremy Atkinson confirms this:

'Across the entire historical sample the authors found that on average, 26.9% of newborns died in their first year of life and 46.2% died before they reached adulthood. Two estimates that are easy to remember: Around a quarter died in the first year of life. Around half died as children. What is striking about the historical estimates is how similar the mortality rates for children were across this very wide range of 43 historical cultures. Whether in Ancient Rome; Ancient Greece; the pre-Columbian Americas; Medieval Japan or Medieval England; the European Renaissance; or Imperial China: Every fourth newborn died in the first year of life. One out of two died in childhood.'[51]

The global infant mortality rate is now 2.9%, but only 1.8% in Japan. What is responsible for this disparity? Magic or science? Very few are likely to say magic. Differences in diet, farming, hygiene, economy, human rights and so on have resulted in this reduction in infant deaths, not magical protection rituals. Yet, millions of three, five, and seven year-old children are taken to this ancient ritual in Japan every year; it's still very common, even after more than 1,500 years, and even taking all the aforementioned into consideration. So, why do people still partake in these festivals? What do they gain from it?

In a series of BBC articles, Alexander Rose, executive director at the Long Now Foundation in San Francisco, remarked on the longevity of

---

51: Volk, Anthony and Atkinson, Jeremy. "Infant and child death in the human environment of evolutionary adaptation," *Evolution and Human Behavior.*

festivals in Japan:

'I witnessed the 66th cycle of a ritual that began more than 13 centuries ago. I watched as Crown Princess Masako led a procession of Shinto priests carrying treasures from the old temple to the new. In Ise, they have been rebuilding the grand Jingū Shrine with wood and thatch every 20 years since at least the seventh century. As part of Shinto ritual, this not only keeps the structures intact even when made out of relatively ephemeral materials, but it allows the master temple builder to train the next generation... Japan is also home to most of the oldest companies in the world, and has a singular affection for maintenance that allows it to sustain structures and rituals for millennia.'[52]

While this certainly holds true for celebrations, the shrine restoration practice Rose highlights is more unusual Other than the special shrines and temples he mentions, it is very difficult to find an old building in Japan. A house only 50 years old is considered ancient. In most towns and cities in the UK, many people live in houses more than 100 years old without thinking of that as anything unusual. The house I grew up in Edinburgh is 120 years old and my family's present house will soon be 200 years old. That's unthinkable in Japan. Old houses and gardens are knocked down here as a matter of course leaving nothing standing at all. This may surprise people to learn, as it doesn't really fit into the image of Japan that many foreigners hold, yet, it's the case. However, Rose's point about rituals certainly holds up. After all, as we have seen with many of the festivals already covered in this book, it's not uncommon for them to stretch back to the eighth century or earlier.

52: Rose, Alexander. "How to build something that lasts 10,000 years." *BBC Future.*

Possibly the most well-known modern Japanese ritual: V fingers up for a photo!

IRO IRO (色々)
(VARIOUS THINGS)

The phrase *iro iro* (色々) in Japanese means 'various things'. This chapter looks at various things that did not fit into the main subjects already focused on.

While the previous chapter highlighted some of the ways in which Western culture has influenced Japan, something we may not be fully aware of is the considerable influence Japanese culture has had on that of the West. For example, it's thought that the word 'Jedi' – of *Star Wars* fame – comes from the Japanese word *jidai* (時代), meaning 'era'. Did Lucas get the pronunciation wrong, or was it deliberately altered in the process of creating the story? Darth Vader's appearance, too, seems partly based on the armor used by Japanese warlords. The inspiration for the Sith seems to have been drawn from *rōnin* (浪人 a wandering samurai who had no lord or master). Even the rebellion of the Satsuma samurai in the 1870s against the imperial forces seems to have been a partial basis for the series. Jediism is now the 7th biggest religion in the UK, largely thanks to the 2001 census in which 177,000 people declared themselves to be Jedi. This will seem ridiculous to some. Indeed, the Charity Commission declared that, in spite of this, it was not to be recognised as a religion: '[the Charity Commission] said there was insufficient evidence that "moral improvement" was central to the beliefs and practices of Jediism and [that it] did not have the "cogency, cohesion, or seriousness" to truly be a belief system. The commission said to be classed as a religion it must also have a positive beneficial impact on society in general and raised concerns that Jediism may, in part, have an "inward focus" on its members.'[53]

53: BBC. "Jedi is not a religion, Charity Commission rules." *BBC News.*

But if we think of Jediism as yet another SOBU, is its creation and spread much different from that of real-world religions? The answer from some might be, 'Yes, very different'; but if we consider that, from a non-partisan perspective, Jedi are just as moral as priests and that the philosophy of the Force is rather analogous to that of Buddhism, and that the ethical training involved in becoming a Jedi is as rigorous as that of most clerical figures, others may reason that, fictitious as *Star Wars* is, it's certainly possible to draw parallel.

Over the course of previous chapters, we've glanced at the relationship between the scientific and the magical several times. The common perception seems to be that these must always exist in opposition; it's my belief, however, that it's entirely possible for them to be complimentary. Let me use the example of the lights hanging above me in this room: we know that scientific study led to an understanding of electricity, which in turn led to the creation of our modern methods of harnessing it for power. This, somewhere along the way, led to the invention of the light-bulb. It's possible for us to know all that while *also* appreciating this marvellous thing from a magical standpoint and giving thanks for it illuminating our homes every day. We can create little rituals to do this. It need not be anything elaborate – we don't need to put on ceremonial clothes, for example – but it could be simple things like saying 'Thanks lads and lassies!' upon switching off the light when we leave the room. That might seem a bit silly, but the point is that such practices serve to focus our awareness of the things around us. It ensures we don't take them for granted, and helps us to develop some measure of understanding of their effect on us, how they help us, how awesome – in the original sense of the word – it is that we have things like light bulbs! (And fires, and stoves, and PCs, and mobile phones and classic Vespa scooters!) It is, at least to my mind, a far better mindset than one that appreciates nothing, takes everything for granted and lacks awareness both of itself and the world around it. The bottom line, though, is that we can both understand and appreciate the scientific practicalities while also practicing a certain type of magical thinking which helps us to increase our understanding of the world and ourselves.

That's not to say that the schools of faith and empiricism have never been at odds. The conflict between traditional ideals and progressive thinking is a long-standing one. In the 12th century Saint Bernard expressed his strong dislike of the teachings of Peter Abelard, a rather radical theologian who attempted to increase the focus on logic and rationalism within theology. It was considered a threat to the foundations of the Church if students were encouraged to form their own opinions. In the Synod of Soissons in 1121, Abelard was found guilty of heresy and his book, *Theologie,* was burned.[54]

Most of us have in our pocket a little machine that makes us more magical than Merlin – our mobile phone. Imagine how astonished our ancestors of centuries past would be at our ability to acquire almost any item of knowledge within seconds, simply by touching the magic tablet in our hands. Imagine how they'd marvel at our ability to speak to someone thousands of miles away. How is it, they might ask, that we are not awestruck by our power to capture the image of a forest or a sunset on these tiny screens? Indeed, how often do we actually reflect on these astonishing powers? Not often. While it's regrettable to think how much of this we take for granted, it's also probably necessary to a certain extent. Imagine if we were constantly, every day, amazed by our phones, or at the way electricity surges along some mysterious line when we throw a switch – we'd never get anything done! So the fact that we tend to take these things for granted as our familiarity with them grows is actually somewhat to our advantage.

However, it seems a shame – even ungrateful – to never wonder at the beauty of a cloud or the flowing of a river. And this is where magical thinking can come in. Through festivals and rituals, we are given occasion to look up at the horizon in wonder: or, as the saying goes, to stare at our navel. As the poetic reflection of the Greek philosopher, Heraclitus notes: 'No man ever steps in the same river twice, for it's not the same river and he's not the same man.'[55] The water of the river you stepped in yesterday has moved on. The river has changed; you have changed. The magic of this concept encourages us to reflect on both our own fluid natures, and the nature of our physical surroundings.

It's true, however, that the Japanese are just as prone to taking things for granted as anyone, despite the widespread belief that East Asian cultures have a deeper connection to nature and a more philosophical bent than those

---

54: Horne, Alistair. *Friend or Foe: a History of France.*
55: Heraclitus of Ephesus, in Plutarch *On the Epsilon at Delphi 392b.*

of Europe. Edward Said in his classic but contentious study Orientalism (1978) explored this image of the mythical Oriental in Western minds and did much to help progress society past this idea. Yet this mistaken impression that the Japanese, Chinese and Koreans are prone to mysterious, superstitious practices persists, which seems nothing short of paradoxical when considered in tandem with the idea of the Japanese not being religious. It is, nonetheless, a seemingly commonplace belief. Naomi Rosenblatt notes the: 'Seemingly contradictory stereotypes of the Middle East, therefore, (as mysterious, alluring, and sumptuous, as well as barbaric, irrational... and "inclined toward despotism"), which were created and developed by American economic and military interactions with the Orient, existed side-by-side in the American popular imagination.'[56] Given, then, that the Japanese have as much of a tendency as anyone to take things such as nature and technology for granted, it stands to reason that they also benefit from the mindfulness of magical thinking. This has an effect on us even if we do not consciously understand it. Pye notes: '...ritual activity is of course accompanied by conceptual assumptions and values which have widespread currency and are taken more or less for granted.'

Possibly the most well-known modern, everyday ritual to have reached the rest of the world from Japan is, of course, the V 'peace' sign, or *piisu sain* (ピースサイン). It's almost mandatory for photos in Japan — the fingers jump up, sometimes on both hands, and out spreads the V sign. Almost everyone in Japan does this, from school girls to grandads. It is a ritual that is *so* commonplace most people would be surprised to hear it called a ritual at all. But that's just what it is, just as much as making the sign of the cross, or bending down to pray towards Mecca. It's a socially meaningful gesture that occurs in certain prescribed times and places; it's symbolic of something. It has socially constructed meaning. Don't be mislead by the fact that it's relatively new — all rituals started sometime, somewhere.

To return to the topic of *jichinsai* (地鎮祭) mentioned in Land Cleansing Rituals, I've spent the last five years investigating the practice of clearing greenery which often accompanies it. In that time I've visited numerous sites,

---

56: Pye, Michael. "Leading Patterns in Everyday Japanese Religion." *Sphinx, Yearbook 2008-9*: p. 45.

taking various before and after photos in the process, and have found that this type of clearance now seems to be standard practice for most construction companies. On average, the lots I studied had around twenty trees or bushes in them prior to redevelopment. In some cases, this was reduced to only one tree or a couple of bushes after construction had finished, though in about two thirds of the plots there was no plant life kept or replanted at all. This means something in the region of a 95% loss of greenery in urban areas. The Ministry of Land, Infrastructure, Transport and Tourism (MLIT) reported that there were a little over 900,000 new houses built across Japan in 2018. Even if we presume that only half of these required the erasure of existing gardens, that still means something in the region of 10 million trees and bushes lost to Japan – every year.

Why have the size and number of gardens declined so much? The Shinto land purification ritual is a long-standing tradition, but was it common practice around, say, the turn of the last century to clear a plot in its entirety when building a new house? Or is this a more recent development? It seems it was more usual to plant a new garden to replace the old one, even as recently as the 1970s; but it's very rare for houses today to have so much as a medium-sized garden. So, what changed? I have put on my Sherlock Holmes hat and tried to find out. Can you 'dig' it, Watson?

Economic factors were among the most commonly cited by people I spoke to, mentioned by both Japanese and long-term foreign residents alike. Many Japanese people, I was told, can't afford to have a garden, both due to the cost of buying land and that of paying a gardener to do maintenance. Another issue is the practice of dividing up an estate between surviving family members, splitting the land into smaller lots and inadvertently destroying greenery in the process. However, this seems to be less of a factor these days than some suppose, as the majority of the sites I have investigated haven't been downsized during redevelopment (sometimes they actually increase in size, with neighboring lots being merged into a single, larger one).

The high price of land during the bubble years of the economy may have been a key influence on the decrease of garden size, however. During this time it became common for estate agents to raze any existing plant life and remove large ornamental stones or ponds to make plots more appealing to lucrative commercial clients. It seems this simply became customary for the sake of convenience and endured. The bubble years were, in fact, quite short-lived (1986 to 1991), meaning we have had almost 30 years of a slow economy; so it's perhaps surprising that the construction industry still engages in practices which seem so out of touch with modern sensibilities.

The fact remains, however, that Japan is a wealthier country today than it has been in the past. If the lack of gardens arises from a lack of means, how is it that so many more Japanese seemed able to afford them in a time when people were less well-off? A possible explanation for this is that most of those older houses with large gardens were owned by those of the middle or upper class, and that the average working-class person in, say, 1930, would have been no more able to afford a garden then than they would now. However, this theory doesn't seem to hold much water either: it seems that wealthier families these days are no more likely than anyone else to keep or replant the previously-existing garden when moving into a new home. This may be in part due to the decline of grandparents living with their children. Some of the people I have spoken to said that caring for the garden was often the jurisdiction of granny and grandad in the past. If fewer grandparents are there to do that, and both parents are working, then it's perhaps a reason why gardens get neglected.

A further nail in the coffin of the affordability argument is that these redeveloped plots are very often still large enough for a garden – even for two or three green areas. Driveways and parking spaces aside, it's common for the remaining land to be left completely empty and concreted over; but surely in these instances it would be possible for some elements of the existing garden to be kept, or for new green areas to be created, without many overheads. It seems, however, that this simply does not happen.

So the next question to ask is: why not do the garden yourself? Gardening is, after all, a popular pastime for many people - one which can be enjoyed without the need for professional services. Why isn't this the case in Japan? It appears to be a matter of convenience. A number of people have told me that gardens are seen as a nuisance – bothersome to look after. Much easier to have empty concrete or pebbles.

None of this is to say that all Japanese people are indifferent to nature, of course. We might say that a continued respect and love for nature is partly what makes this practice so jarring Ironically, the reason for it may be precisely *because* Japanese people hold nature in such high regard. A lawyer in Nagoya told me: 'Some people consider it to be disrespectful not to look after trees and plants, but since they don't have enough time they think it's better not to have a garden at all.'

As with anything, outlooks will differ. While most are content to concrete over gardens, others seek to do otherwise. I was recently delighted to notice a man in his 30s happily working on a new garden, by himself, DIY-style. He told me that the property which had previously occupied the lot had belonged to his grandparents, and that after building the new house there he had decided to rebuild most of the garden, too. He expressed disappointment that more people did not do the same. The next week I saw his whole family out laying a new lawn.

Even the coronavirus crisis has been connected with green issues. A recent article in Forbes magazine described an alarming link between deforestation and viruses: 'Scientists have been warning that deforestation may be creating an accidental laboratory for the emergence of new viruses in environments that have been disturbed by humans. In the wake of HIV, Ebola and SARS, scientists documented a potential path for viruses from bats through other mammals to humans. Some scientists and doctors have further argued that path is paved by deforestation.'[57]

Not only is this bad for the environment, it's bad for people too. Various studies have confirmed the link between green space and health, such as a study in the Netherlands, that concluded: 'This research shows that the percentage of green space in people's living environment has a positive association with the perceived general health of residents. Green space seems to be more than just a luxury and consequently the development of green space should be allocated a more central position in spatial planning policy.'[58] An interesting connected point is that in Japan it is common for the makers of a new house to go around to the nearest neighbours, politely introduce themselves, with a small gift and apologise for the noise of the construction. That's nice, but surely an apology for having decreased the beauty and health of the area by cutting down all those lovely old trees and flowers should also be included, no?

In pursuing economic measures we also need to take into account the physical history of areas, the natural beauty, the environment and our

57: McMahon, Jeff. "How Deforestation Drives the Emergence of Novel Coronaviruses." *Forbes.*
58: Maas J, Verheij R.A., et al. "Green space, urbanity, and health: how strong is the relation?." *Journal of Epidemiology and Community Health.*

health. Surely even the most rampant capitalist thinks those things are of some importance? As an example of how the economic system is involved in the destruction of these in Japan an expert in the subject reminded me that the land cleansing ceremonies are a considerable source of funding for local Shinto shrines. If they refused to conduct it because the company involved was destroying nature they would lose income. To put it bluntly then, what they are involved in is the sanctification of the destruction of nature.

CONCLUSION

Over the course of this book we have considered the ins and outs of various festivals, rituals and acts, all of which appear to contradict the following assertion: 'the Japanese are not religious'. Both the sheer number of such practices and philosophies and the high percentage of Japanese people who partake in them clearly show this idea to be incorrect. It just ain't true. At least, not according to the definition of 'religion' – or 'magic' – that this book sets forward, that is. I introduced the umbrella term 'SOBU' in the introduction, 'Systems of Organisation, Behaviour, Understanding', and examined the ways in which these SOBU affect our understanding and outlook on the world and our place in it. We have also looked at a wide range of celebrations, ceremonies and magical practices and the particulars thereof, many of these beautifully illustrated by UK-based artist Fumio Obata. This is our second collaboration on a long book.

With all this in mind, this is perhaps a good moment to have a look at some statistics. A Statista study on religions in Japan claimed that: 'In 2017, around 70% of the total population of Japan participated in Shinto practices. Closely behind is Buddhism, with more than 69% of the population adhering to its practices. Most Japanese thus practice both religions.'[59] While these are certainly impressively high percentages, it's worth noting the distinction between participation and being a practicing member of a faith. It's possible that these figures also include people who only participate in Shinto or Buddhist ceremonies a few times a year – during the rituals outlined in this book – and are otherwise secular in their day-to-day lives.

A World Values Survey found that 88% of Japanese say they are not active in a church, and that 76% say they are not religious/did not have a religious upbringing. This seems directly contradictory, then, to the findings

---

59: Statista. "Religious affiliation in Japan 2017."

of the Statista survey. The same study offers a way to reconcile this, however, as Rodney Stark tells us: 'The majority (57%) believe in the supernatural. Almost two-thirds (63%) believe that humans have souls... the Japanese turn out to be deeply and very actively religious if unchurched religion and spirituality are examined.'[60]

The distinguishing factor of 'unchurched religion' is a vital one, then. Adherence to Shinto and Buddhist religions (in Japan, at least) does not present via the same hallmarks as many Abrahamic religions, which leads it to being mistaken for a lack of religion. One commentator in the magazine *Japan Today* summarised this perfectly: '... to me, a Catholic who goes to church every Sunday, I thought that anyone who didn't go to church on Sunday could not be considered "religious." Back then, my conclusion was that Japanese could not possibly be religious... [but] We are missing the point when we compare Japanese religious beliefs to those of Christianity, Islam etc. a far better point of comparison would be with the many pantheistic religions which also have no central authority'[61].

Foreign visitors often talk about the 'magic' of Japan. What do people really mean when they say that? Are they simply parroting a shallow cliché? Do most foreigner visitors really see and feel the magic they're referring to? Come to that, are most Japanese themselves aware of the symbolism and history of the rituals they take part in, and do they take them 'seriously'? This reminds me of the lyrics to a song by The Who: 'I've got values, but I don't know how or why'[62]. So what effect can these things have, if any, if people don't even know the how or why of the magic?

There is an infamous story told about Nobel Prize winner Niels Bohr, the atomic scientist. A visiting friend of his was surprised to notice a horseshoe hanging over his door. Unable to contain his incredulity, he said:

'Niels, it can't possibly be that you, a brilliant scientist, believe that foolish horseshoe superstition!'

'Of course not...but I understand it's lucky whether you believe in it or not.'[63]

How can such magic 'work' even if we don't believe in it? Or, how can it work if we have little understanding of the original symbolism, or

60: Stark, Rodney. *Exploring the Religious Life.*
61: *Japan Today.* "How religious are Japanese people?"
62: The Who, and Townshend, Pete. "The Seeker."
63: Nils Bohr in Kenyon, E.E.. "The Wit Parade," *San Francisco Examiner.*

when or where the ritual started? Two possible ideas come to mind: that the magic has an objective power outside of our view and practice of it. The other possibility is that the rituals and festivals and practises can perform their basic function even without our conscious knowledge of their origin and symbolism. Perhaps they have an effect on an unconscious level. Or perhaps the effect is largely because of taking part in a group. Japanese people still go to their local shrine, even if few people know when the practice started. The basic act of going there, with friends and family, on Dec 31st, a sliver before midnight, has an effect. We decorate the Christmas tree around early December with our loved ones, even if we don't know the history behind the tradition. The yearly ritual of dusting down the box of decorations, taking out this shiny bauble, that snowman, the fairy for the top of the tree serves to tell us: 'This is a special time'. And whether you celebrate the holiday as a religious or a secular one – as Bohr noted – the magic works regardless. Christmas is a meaningful occasion, one way or another. In just the same way, the burning of last year's charms in the New Year fires is something special, even if we don't believe in Shintoism or Buddhism.

Charles Baudelaire wrote in 1854: 'The beauty of Paris is all around us, but we don't see it.'[64] As we've already observed, an effective way to restore awareness of the things around us is to think magically. Baudelaire wrote of the flâneur who strolls around trying to see and experience Paris beyond what the rest of the blinkered, work-focused world sees – using poetry as a way of both experiencing and expressing more deeply. Through the magic of the arts, we bring the world – or at least our consciousness of it – into existence. To quote yet another insightful writer, Henry Miller: 'Every moment is a golden one for him who has the vision to recognize it as such.'[65]

Despite the weightiness of these ideas, both Western and Eastern magical traditions also recognise the importance of humour and flexibility as positive human qualities and allow room for them to surface during more serious proceedings. One cute example which comes to mind occurred when an uncle in my son's Japanese family died. My son was only about two years old at the time. A solemn Buddhist ritual of ancient origin was performed in the uncle's old house and various members of the family participated, dressed in black. My son was sitting on my knee, and while the Buddhist priest

---

64: Baudelaire, Charles. *The Painter of Modern Life And Other Essays.*
65: Miller, Henry. *The World of Sex.*

chanted the age-old prayers to the dead my son... farted. Loudly. *Phhuuuu...* But he did it at the exact moment there was a break in the chanting. Everyone sniggered and then tried to put a serious face back on. Afterwards, I was a bit nervous and apologised to the priest, but he just smiled and said 'It was good timing'. Ha!

The main takeaway from all of this is that, by becoming more actively open to and aware of magic, you also begin to actively gain more knowledge about the world around you. You start to become interested in how things work and evolve. You may look up where Halloween came from and find that it's connected to the ancient Celtic festival *Samhain* of Irish and Scottish origin. You may discover the Chinese origins of a lantern festival held in your town. You may find out that the tree in your grandmother's garden is actually connected to a fertility ritual. Magical education!

But what form might magical practices take in the future? How will technological development affect our rituals, ceremonies and festivals? A private student of mine is a computer scientist at a big corporation here in Japan, and he recently told me about how they are developing a type of hololens system which allows people wearing pairs of special smart glasses to view holographic 3D images. This has the interesting title of 'mixed reality technology' – a term which implies that reality can be mixed, manipulated and interfaced with. Sounds quite a lot like magic to me.

So what would be the point of buying a charm to protect against, say, earthquakes if an alarm on your smartphone will offer a far more reliable safeguard? And if the intertwining of our own neural networks with those of computer systems continues to develop, then surely an astonishing realisation of the power of our consciousness to affect change in the world won't be far behind. Where will that leave simple, old-fashioned objects like the *hamaya* arrow or festivals like *Hanami*? Will they become so outdated and unnecessary as to be forgotten? Evidence thus far suggests otherwise. Attendance of *Hanami* hasn't declined because almost everyone there has a cell phone in their pocket. If there's one thing that is abundantly clear about Japanese magical practices, it is how well they have endured. And while some degree of change is all but inevitable, their longevity is a testament to their adaptability.

The recent implementation of making e-payments to shrines via means such as Paypal is a perfect example of this adaptability in action. But change, no matter how innovative, is usually slow to take effect, and such methods are still seen as less respectful – less 'magical'. A report in *Kyōdō News* in 2019 said: 'But many visitors still feel uncomfortable offering e-money, according to Nikkō Futarasan shrine, a World Heritage site in Tochigi Prefecture, north of Tokyo. It started accepting offerings through PayPal early February, but most worshippers headed for its offering box, saying the act of throwing coins itself has a meaning to them.'[66] People remarked that they felt online payments would bring them less good fortune. It's this sort of logic that provides us with a good indication that the old-fashioned, face-to-face, touch-the-stone magical experience will continue despite technological development.

Another glimpse of the future may be found in the way certain religious groups react to disasters. Levi McLaughlin from the Department of Philosophy and Religious Studies at North Carolina State University conducted some research into this. He found that religious aid workers are usually found on the front lines of Japanese social welfare provision in times of crisis. Buddhist priests he spoke to told him: 'We are gathering supplies from volunteers at the temple, from parishioners and their families, to help those who are afflicted by difficulties that result from the call to self-restraint...' McLaughlin concludes that the efforts of people like Reverend Asahikawa provide an exemplary model of the way in which Japan's religious activists combine a focus on otherworldly enlightenment with practical responses to everyday challenges such as viruses, floods and earthquakes, drawing on: 'age-old rituals as they initiate new means of meeting present-day needs'.[67]

A related question is: how will an increased foreign-born population affect Japanese magical practices? The number of foreigners living in Japan is still very small, but it is slowly growing. So, it could be that these foreigners will not learn certain Japanese customs or will bring in their own; though we may make the point that, if this were to be the case, it would hardly be the first time this has happened. The point of origin for what are considered to be very 'Japanese' festivals and rituals is often China and India, even if it was more than 1,000 years ago. Halloween and Christmas, too, are a recent adoptions from Western countries. There are no unchanging rituals and

66: *Kyodo News*. "Worshippers not buying cashless offerings at Japanese temples and shrines."
67: McLaughlin, Levi. "Japanese Religious Responses to COVID-19: A Preliminary Report." *Asia Pacific Journal.*

festivals that last forever; there are just different ages and certain stages. We can also observe that foreigners who live in Japan for many years develop a strong interest in taking part in local culture and that often the people who are most keen on Japanese-style gardens are Westerners. Given the rapid rate at which gardens are being destroyed in Japan, it may even come to the point that the best way to tell if a house belongs to a foreigner is to look at how Japanese the garden is!

As they say in Japanese, *sono uchi ni wakaru* (そのうちに分かる), eventually we will see. I think it's highly likely that some form of religious or magical thinking, alongside scientific advances, will continue to help us to see and to understand both ourselves and the environment. And that festivals and rituals will persist as a form of symbolic glue for community and social connections. Therefore, I will conclude this book with the claim that the sum total of all these rituals, festivals and practices means that the vast majority of the 125 million people living in Japan engage in what can be called magical acts and thinking... or religion, if you prefer. The benefit of this can be found and felt in everything from community feeling and individual's sense of themselves, to marking periods in our lives; as a spur to the imagination, to creativity; even in our relationship with nature and the very flow of existence. These things are basic, and they are vital. Magical acts and thinking do something for us, in Japan and all over the world.

BIBLIOGRAPHY AND
FURTHER READING

Baudelaire, Charles. *The Painter of Modern Life And Other Essays*. Cambridge: Da Capo Press, 1986.

BBC. "Jedi is not a religion, Charity Commission rules." *BBC News*, 9 December 2016. https://www.bbc.com/news/uk-38368526

Boret, Sébastien Penmellen. *Japanese Tree Burial: Ecology, Kinship and the Culture of Death*. Abingdon-on-Thames: Routledge, 2014.

Bradshaw, Alex. Interview by author, October, 2020.

Chavez, Amy. *Guide to Best Behavior in Japan: Do It Right and Be Polite!* Berkeley: Stone Bridge Press, 2018.

Chavez, Amy. "Five things you need to know about Obon." *Japan Today*, 11 August 2015. https://japantoday.com/category/features/five-things-you-need-to-know-about-obon

Durkheim, Emile. *The Elementary Forms of the Religious Life*. London: George Allen & Unwin Ltd, 1915.

Decker, Kevin and Eberl, Jason. *Star Wars and Philosophy: More Powerful than You Can Possibly Imagine*. Chicago: Open Court, 2005.

DeHart, Jonathan. *Moon Japan: Plan Your Trip, Avoid the Crowds, and Experience the Real Japan*. New York: Moon Travel, 2020.

de Waal, Frans. *The Bonobo and the Atheist: In Search of Humanism Among the Primates*. New York: W. W. Norton & Company, 2014.
DK Eyewitness. *Be More Japan: The Art of Japanese Living*. London: DK Eyewitness, 2019.

Elson, Angela. "The Japanese Art of Grieving a Miscarriage." *New York Times*, 6 January 2017. https://www.nytimes.com/2017/01/06/well/family/the-japanese-art-of-grieving-a-miscarriage.html

Erlbach, Matthew-Lee. "We Are the Champions". *Netflix Original Series*, Episode 1, November 2020.

Harari, Yuval Noah. *Sapiens: A Brief History of Humankind*. London: Harvill Secker, 2011.

Hayman, Ronald. K: *A Biography of Kafka*. London: Phoenix Press, 1981.

Heraclitus of Ephesus (c. 535 – c. 475 BC), in Plutarch *On the Epsilon at Delphi* 392b, c. 100AD.

Horii, Mitsutoshi. "Critical Reflections on the Religious-Secular Dichotomy in Japan," in *Making Religion: Theory and Practice in the Discursive Study of Religion*, Wijsen, Frans and von Stuckrad, Kocku (eds). Leiden: Brill, 2016.

Horne, Alistair. *Friend or Foe: a History of France*. London: Weidenfeld & Nicolson, 2004.

Japan Today. "How religious are Japanese people?" *Japan Today*, 27 October 2013. https://japantoday.com/category/features/opinions/how-religious-are-japanese-people

Jacobsen, Natalie. "Japanese Lucky Charms: A Guide to Omamori." *Tokyo Weekender*, 13 May 2015. https://www.tokyoweekender.com/2015/05/japanese-lucky-charms-the-guide-to-omamori

Kaikita, Yukiko. Interview by author, January 2020.

Kasahara, K. (ed.) *Nippon no Rekishi (The History of Japan)*. Tokyo: Kodansha, 1995.

Kaveney, Roz. "Alan Moore: Could it be magic?" *The Independent*, 4 November 2005. https://www.independent.co.uk/arts-entertainment/books/features/alan-moore-could-it-be-magic-324487.html

Kenyon, E.E. "The Wit Parade." *San Francisco Examiner*, 29 September 1957.

Kimura, Hiroko. Interview by author, March 2020.

Kokugakuin University. Encyclopedia of Shinto. "Jōtōsai." 24 February 2007. http://eos.kokugakuin.ac.jp/modules/xwords/entry.php

Koloa Jodo Mission. "Meaning of Hanabi – A Brief History of Fireworks in Japan."

7 July 2020. https://www.koloajodo.com/2020/07/07/meaning-of-hanabi-a-brief-history-of-fireworks-in-japan

Kyodo News. "Worshippers not buying cashless offerings at Japanese temples and shrines." *Kyodo News*, 28 February 2019. https://english.kyodonews.net/news/2019/02/cd4d661b3dd8-worshippers-divided-over-e-money-offerings-at-japanese-temples.html

LeFebvre, Jesse. "Christian Wedding Ceremonies—"Nonreligiousness" in Contemporary Japan." *Japanese Journal of Religious Studies* 42/2: 185–203, 2015.

Maas, J., Verheij, R.A., Groenewegen, P.P., de Vries, S., and Spreeuwenberg, P. "Green space, urbanity, and health: how strong is the relation?." *Journal of Epidemiology and Community Health*, 60/7: 587☐592, 2006.

Marfording, Annette. "Cultural Relativism and the construction of culture: An examination of Japan," *Human Rights Quarterly*, 19/2 431-448, 1997.

Masumizu, Haruka. "A guide to New Year traditions in Japan." *Japan Today*, 30 December 2017. https://japantoday.com/category/features/lifestyle/new-year-traditions-in-japan
McLaughlin, Levi. "Japanese Religious Responses to COVID-19: A Preliminary Report." *Asia Pacific Journal*, 18/9: 3, May 2020.

McMahon, Jeff. "How Deforestation Drives the Emergence of Novel Coronaviruses." *Forbes*, 21 March 2020. https://www.forbes.com/sites/jeffmcmahon/2020/03/21/how-deforestation-is-driving-the-emergence-of-novel-coronaviruses

Meleen, Michele. "Native American Death Rituals." *Love to Know*, undated. https://dying.lovetoknow.com/native-american-death-rituals

Miller, Henry. *The World of Sex*. New York: Grove Press, 1965.

Moore, Alan and Campbell, Eddie. *From Hell*. Georgia: Top Shelf Productions, 2016.

Noren, Anders. "Journey of Otemoyan (おてもやん) and the Writer of the Song, the Most Famous Folk Song in Kumamoto." *Untapped Kumamoto*, 19 July 2020. https://untappedkumamoto.com/history-culture/3173

Payne, Richard K. "The Ritual Culture of Japan: Symbolism, Ritual and the Arts," in *Nanzan Guide to Japanese Religions*, Swanson, Paul and Chilson, Clark (eds). Honolulu: University of Hawaii Press, 2006: p. 246.

Powell, Richard R. (2004). *Wabi Sabi Simple*. Avon, MA: Adams Media, 2004.

Pye, Michael. "Leading Patterns in Everyday Japanese Religion." *Sphinx, Yearbook 2008-9 (Societas Scientiarum Fennica)*, 2009: p. 45.

Pye, Michael. "The Structure of Religious Systems in Contemporary Japan: Shinto Variations on Buddhist Pilgrimage." *Occasional Papers of the Centre for Japanese Studies*, University of Marburg, No. 30: 2007.

Pye, Michael. "Rationality, Ritual and Life-shaping Decisions in Modern Japan." *Occasional Papers of the Centre for Japanese Studies*, University of Marburg, No. 29: 2003.

Rots, Aike P. "Sacred Forests, Sacred Nation: The Shinto Environmentalist Paradigm and the Rediscovery of 'Chinju no Mori'." *Japanese Journal of Religious Studies*, 42/2: 2015.

Rambelli, Fabio (ed). *Spirits and Animism in Contemporary Japan: the Invisible Empire*. London: Bloomsbury, 2019.

Rambelli, Fabio. "True Words, Silence, and the Adamantine Dance." *Japanese Journal of Religious Studies*, 21/4: 1994.

Reed, William. Interview by author, November 2020.

Renfrew, Colin and Morley, Iain (eds). *Becoming Human: Innovation in Prehistoric Material and Spiritual Cultures*. Cambridge: Cambridge University Press, 2009: pp. 159-75.

Renshaw, Steve and Ihara, Saori. "The Lunar Calendar in Japan." *Rensha Works*. February 2010. http://www.renshaworks.com/jastro/calendar.htm

Rose, Alexander. "How to build something that lasts 10,000 years." *BBC Future*, 11 June 2019. https://www.bbc.com/future/article/20190611-how-to-build-something-that-lasts-10000-years

Rosenblatt, Naomi. "Orientalism in American Popular Culture." *Penn History Review*, Issue 2, Spring 2009: p. 54.

Salman, Mac. "Need a break from a stressful boss? Try taking him to karaoke." *Linkedin*, 7 September 2020. https://www.linkedin.com/pulse/need-break-from-stressful-boss-try-taking-him-karaoke-duncan-bartlett

Scheffler, A.O. and Scheffler, P.P. *CalMaster2000: Dates, Holidays, and*

Astronomical Events. Pittsburgh, PA: Zephyr Services, 1991.

Shields, James Mark. "Beyond Belief: Japanese Approaches to the Meaning of Religion." *Studies in Religion / Sciences religieuses*, 39/2: 2010: p. 5.

Statistics Bureau of Japan. "Statistical Handbook of Japan 2020". *Statistics Bureau of Japan*, 2020. https://www.stat.go.jp/english/index.html

Statista. "Religious affiliation in Japan 2017." 16 September 2020. https://www.statista.com/statistics/237609/religions-in-japan/

Stark, Rodney. *Exploring the Religious Life*. Baltimore: JHU Press, 2004.

Sugimoto, Mayayoshi, and Swain, David L. *Science and Culture in Traditional Japan*. Tokyo: Charles E. Tuttle Co. Inc, 1989.

Traditional Kyoto. "Lions – Komainu." *Traditional Kyoto*, undated. https://traditionalkyoto.com/culture/figures/lions-komainu

Thomas, Baraka Jolyon. *Drawing on Tradition: Manga, Anime and Religion in Contemporary Japan*. Honolulu: University of Hawaii, 2020.

Thomas, Russell. "Hatsuhinode: Where to see the first sunrise of the decade." *The Japan Times*, 28 December 2019. https://www.japantimes.co.jp/life/2019/12/28/travel/hatsuhinode-first-sunrise-decade-around-tokyo

Trezise, Simon (ed). *The Cambridge Companion to French Music*. Cambridge: Cambridge University Press, 2015: p. 350.

Turner, Victor, and Yamaguchi, Masao (eds). *Misetnono no jirtruigaku* 見世物の人類学 *Spectacle—An Anthropological Inquiry*. Tokyo: Sanseido, 1983.

Turner, Victor. *The Ritual Process: Structure and Anti-Structure*. Chicago: Aldine Publishing, 1969.
Wada, Teni. "Setsubun (節分): The Japanese Festival of Bean Throwing and Sushi Rolling," *Kokoro Cares*, undated. https://kokorocares.com/blogs/blog/setsubun-節分-the-japanese-festival-of-bean-throwing-and-sushi-rolling

The Who, and Townshend, Pete. "The Seeker." The Seeker, Track, 1970, non-album single.

Wikipedia. "Communitas." *Wikipedia*, undated. https://en.wikipedia.org/wiki/Communitas

Wilson, Sean Michael. "Japan: surprisingly, sensibly and endearingly low-tech." *The Japan Times*, 25 Nov 2015. https://www.japantimes.co.jp/community/2015/11/25/voices/japan-surprisingly-sensibly-endearingly-low-tech

Wilson, Sean Michael. "Undokai and Anarchism." *Japan Daily*, 8 September 2015. https://japandaily.jp/undokai-and-anarchism-1905

Wilson, Sean Michael. "Dispatches from the Kumamoto quake zone." *The Japan Times*, 20 April 2016. https://www.japantimes.co.jp/community/2016/04/20/issues/dispatches-kumamoto-quake-zone.

Wilson, Sean Michael. "With every new construction in Japan, fewer trees." *The Japan Times*, 20 September 2017. https://www.japantimes.co.jp/community/2017/09/20/voices/every-new-construction-japan-less-trees

Volk, Anthony and Atkinson, Jeremy. "Infant and child death in the human environment of evolutionary adaptation," *Evolution and Human Behavior*, 34/3: May 2013.

Virág, Curie. *The Emotions in Early Chinese Philosophy*. Oxford: Oxford University Press, 2017: p. 182.

Yoneyama, Shoko, "Rethinking Human-Nature Relationships in the Time of Coronavirus: Postmodern Animism in Films by Miyazaki Hayao & Shinkai Makoto." *Asia Pacific Journal*, 18/16:6, 15 August 2020.